Mastering Self-Leadership

Empowering Yourself for Personal Excellence

Charles C. Manz, Ph.D.

PRENTICE HALL, Englewood Cliffs, New Jersey 07632

Library of Congress Cataloging-in-Publication Data

Manz, Charles C.
    Mastering self-leadership : empowering yourself for personal
    excellence / Charles C. Manz.
            p.   cm.
    Includes index.
    ISBN 0-13-560863-5
    1. Leadership.   I. Title.
HD57.7.M387   1991   91-26493
303.3'4--dc20   CIP

Acquisitions editor: John Willig
Production editor: Elaine Lynch
Copy editor: Mary Louise Byrd
Cover designer: Bruce Kenselaar
Pre-press buyer: Mary McCartney
Manufacturing buyer: Susan Brunke

 Published by Prentice-Hall, Inc.
A Simon & Schuster Company
Englewood Cliffs, New Jersey 07632

An earlier version of this book was published, by Prentice Hall, with the
title *The Art of Self-Leadership.*

The publisher offers discounts on this book when ordered
in bulk quantities. For more information, write:

Special Sales/College Marketing
Prentice-Hall, Inc.
College Technical and Reference Division
Englewood Cliffs, NJ 07632

Printed in the United States of America
10 9 8 7 6 5 4 3

ISBN 0-13-560863-5

Prentice-Hall International (UK) Limited, *London*
Prentice-Hall of Australia Pty. Limited, *Sydney*
Prentice-Hall Canada Inc., *Toronto*
Prentice-Hall Hispanoamericana, S.A., *Mexico*
Prentice-Hall of India Private Limited, *New Delhi*
Prentice-Hall of Japan, Inc., *Tokyo*
Simon & Schuster Asia Pte. Ltd., *Singapore*
Editora Prentice-Hall do Brasil, Ltda., *Rio de Janeiro*

To Karen, Mom, and Dad
    the three people who contributed the most
    to my acquisition of self-leadership
    sufficient to write this book.

Charles C. Manz, Ph.D., is an associate professor of management in the Department of Management, Arizona State University, Tempe, Arizona 85287. He was a recipient of the prestigious Marvin Bower Fellowship at Harvard Business School 1988-1989 "awarded for outstanding achievement in business scholarship... for the quality and quantity of his published work" on self-managing work teams and employee self-leadership. He is co-author of SuperLeadership: Leading Others to Lead Themselves (Prentice Hall, 1989; Berkley, paperback, 1990), which won the National Stybel-Peabody Prize for best book of the year. He serves as a consultant and speaker on leadership, self-management, and work teams for many organizations including Fortune 500 companies.

Contents

Preface

"I can do it!" he shouted at the figure across the room. "All my life you've been holding me back, beating me down—I've had it!" "Why? Why can't you just let me be? I could really be somebody," he continued, now in a pleading voice.

For a while he was quiet except for the sound of his own deep breathing. He just stared at what he now realized was his ultimate adversary. The figure was still; it said nothing. "Oh, God," he sighed. He shifted his gaze to the bright lights of the city below. Beginning to see the possibilities for his life, he felt a surge of excitement, of potential purpose, go through his every fiber.

He was lost somewhere in his imagination for what seemed several minutes. Suddenly reality hit him squarely and coldly again. His sense of possible escape was lost. He felt the chains weighing heavy on his soul. And he returned his gaze slowly, steadily, helplessly to the figure of his oppressor. Once more he looked squarely into the eyes of the figure in the mirror before him.

This book is about self-leadership. It emphasizes that we choose what we are and what we become. It recognizes that the world does not always cooperate with our goals, but that we largely create that personal world with which we must cope. It also points out that we influence our actions in countless ways, which we may not even be aware of.

The world is experiencing a knowledge explosion. It is frightening to realize that what we learn often becomes obsolete in a short time. What doesn't change, however, is our need to deal effectively with this complex world and to lead ourselves to fulfillment in life. If we can develop the ability to renew ourselves continually and to overcome our obstacles on our way to life's exhilarations, we can become what we choose for ourselves.

This is *not* another book about leadership. Unfortunately, when I mention the topic of self-leadership to others, many simply lump it in the leadership category. This tendency emphasizes why *self*-leadership is so important. *Self*-leadership includes what has more frequently been called self-management, and more. It addresses what has been referred to as the "missing link in managerial effectiveness" and "the ultimate source of behavioral control."* Too often we focus on ways to influence others and neglect the more fundamental issue of how we can better lead ourselves toward our personal goals and dreams. Our society has been especially good at fostering a sense of external control and "other responsibility" in persons. The increasing role of government in so many areas of our personal lives and welfare that were once considered individual responsibilities is a salient symptom of this trend.

Recently, however, significant efforts have been made to place an increased emphasis on personal control and responsibility of workers in organizations. Recent popularity of management techniques such as quality circles, self-managing work groups or teams, Japanese management systems, and so forth are indicative of this growing emphasis on employee participation. The self-managed team approach in particular has been extensively used as a new management approach across a wide range of industries and work settings in both manufacturing and service organizations. Trends such as these point to the importance of developing stronger self-management, as opposed to "management of others," capability in people. Managers and professionals, who often have a great deal of responsibility, freedom, and discretion concerning how they perform their jobs, always have had a particularly acute need for effective self-leadership practice.

My primary purpose in presenting the ideas on the following pages is to address these needs. That is, this book is designed to be a first step in providing a framework for assisting readers to work on their own self-leadership. It can be a valuable tool for helping workers and people in general in their personal lives to master personal self-management skills and beyond. Self-assessment questionnaires, checklists, and exercises are included specifically

---

*Fred Luthans and Tim R. V. Davis, "Behavioral Self-Management—The Missing Link in Managerial Effectiveness," *Organizational Dynamics*, (Summer 1979), 42–60; and Charles C. Manz, "A Proposed Model of Self-Management: The Underlying Source of Behavioral Control," *Proceedings: Southern Management Association*, Atlanta, 1981.

for this purpose. I have identified the topic of this book as "self-leadership," as opposed to "self-management" or "self-control" or some other label, in the hope that it will create a positive image in the mind of the reader. Being effective self-leaders is more than just getting ourselves to do what we are told or to do those important things that we have put off doing. It involves redesigning our work and our world (both our physical world and the world we carry around in our thoughts), to the extent possible, so that they bring out our best qualities and our fullest potential. It involves more than just dragging ourselves through the performance of necessary tasks; instead, it involves each of us truly being our own ultimate leader.

I continually witness instances in which people experience a strong sense of failure because they fall well short of the goals and dreams they have set for their lives. Their failure can invariably be traced, at least in part, to shortcomings of their own self-leadership. This book represents an attempt to help persons avoid this fate. The ideas presented are largely based on research in psychology and human management. The book was originally envisioned as appealing to a worker, manager, and professional market, but its scope is really much greater: It's for every person who wants to become more than what he or she is at present. It is written in the hope that you will become the self-leader you are capable of becoming and that you might help others to do the same.

ACKNOWLEDGMENTS

As with most worthwhile projects, there are a great many people who have contributed significantly to this book. In particular, I would like to thank Hank Sims for his collegial support of me and my work over the past few years. I also want to extend thanks to many other colleagues for their support and encouragement. Junior Feild, Bill Holley, and Art Bedeian provided especially important support to me at the beginning stages of this manuscript. Also, discussions with Kevin Mossholder, Bill Giles, Chris Neck, and Kerry Davis, among others, provided me with valuable food for thought during my writing. I would like to thank Denny Gioia as well for insightful exchanges and suggestions.

I gratefully acknowledge the special inspiration I have received from the work, ideas, and thoughtful encouragement of

Richard Hackman, Ed Lawler, Chris Argyris, Fred Luthans, Ted Levitt, Rosabeth Moss Kanter, Richard Walton, and John Kotter.

In addition, I want to express my appreciation to the folks at Prentice Hall for their assistance in converting my ideas into a book. I want to extend a special thanks to Ted Arnold without whose encouragement and suggestions regarding the publication process this book might never have found its way to publication.

I also want to express my gratitude to my family for their patience during my long hours spent under lamplight writing away. I especially want to thank my wife, Karen, who in her own way contributed to the ideas in this book through our many discussions of the material, her patient listening to yet another newly written passage of the book's content, and her usually diplomatic suggestions for various changes in the text. Finally, I want to thank Mike Mahoney, who helped provide direction and shape to my growing desire to explore the realms of the vast potential locked in each living person—especially those who have the good or bad fortune of having to work for a living.

1

The Journey

He set out on the journey with the best of intentions and with true determination. He would discover the place of peace, contentment, and fulfillment. This wonderful land was out there: He would find it, and then return to his hopeful, hard-working people and bring them, too. Then all would at last be released from their toil-laden and imperfect existence.

He traveled long and hard; he crossed vast deserts and the highest of snow-capped mountains; he fought with wild beasts and defended himself against strange and hostile peoples. Still he could not find the wonderful land for which he searched.

At last, one day many years later, he wearily entered a land that seemed somehow peaceful. It was pleasant to look upon, and yes, the people were quite friendly. Somehow the land seemed new, yet comfortably familiar. He enjoyed himself for several days while he recovered from his long travels and regained his clarity of perspective.

Then one morning, having significantly recovered his faculties, the strangest of sensations went through him. This land had seemed familiar because it was the home that he had left behind so many years before. The people had not recognized him because of his greatly increased age and weather-worn features. Once realizing who he was, they were in a state of excitement and curiosity to know of the wonderful land of peace, contentment, and fulfillment that he must surely have discovered after so many years. They had waited so long for his return so that they too, might go there. Slowly the man responded to their questions. "Yes," he said, "there is a wonderful land and I have discovered it. It is not as I thought, though. You see, to go there is to be *here*—we were there all along but did not see."

"Well then, you have wasted many years and our hopes have been in vain," the people cried. "And look at you—you are but a shell of the fine physical specimen you were when you left."

"It is true," said the man. "I have traded many years of my life and a large portion of my physical strength for the realization that the wonderful land I sought in vain was mine all along. But I say to you, it is the best exchange I have ever made. You too can enjoy the contentment that I now know if you will but travel, not foolishly as I did, but with your mind into your heart so that you might know your soul."

This book represents a journey. It is about why we are what we are and why we do what we do. It is a journey with the destination of a better understanding of ourselves and obtainment of an increased potential to lead ourselves to our own goals. It is a journey into the imagination, and yet into the most real aspects of life. It is a fascinating journey and a very worthwhile one. This book is about the journey of life, and it is for you.... Happy travels!

LEADERSHIP

This is not a book about leadership of others. Instead, it is about something more fundamental and more powerful—*self*-leadership. It is about the leadership that we exercise over ourselves. In fact, if we ever hope to be effective leaders of others, we need first to be able to effectively lead ourselves. To understand better the process of self-leadership and how we can improve our capability in this area, it is useful first to explore the meaning of the term *leadership*.

There are a seemingly endless number of definitions and descriptions of leadership—largely as a result of the vast number of persons who have researched and written on the subject (and the equal vastness of their different viewpoints). One of the most widely recognized names associated with the topic is the now deceased Ralph M. Stogdill. Dr. Stogdill authored a handbook of leadership, published in 1974, which reviewed theory and research on the subject. Since that time this book has been revised by Bernard M. Bass, most recently in 1990.[1] The book has pointed out that leadership has been conceived of in many ways, including the art of inducing compliance; a personality concept; a form of persuasion; a set of acts or behaviors; an instrument of goal achievement; an effect of group interaction; a differentiated role;

and the exercise of influence. All of these descriptions have some merit. The most useful definition of leadership, to focus on the idea of self-leadership, however, is simply "a process of influence." This short definition is a broad and meaningful one that recognizes both the importance of human influence in determining what we are and what we do and the complexity involved (that is, that influence takes place not as an isolated event, but as a process involving many parts).

The existing literature on leadership is almost universally focused on influence exercised by one or more persons over others (in other words, influence exercised by "leaders" on others). In undertaking a journey toward achievement of an understanding and improvement of our own self-leadership, the first step involved is recognizing that leadership is not just an outward process; that is, we can and do lead ourselves.

SOURCES OF LEADERSHIP

Leadership (the process of influence) can originate from a number of sources. The most commonly recognized source of leadership, of course, involves the influence leaders exercise over their followers. This is also the most externally oriented view of leadership. It does not recognize the influence that we exercise on ourselves. An example of this external view is the giving of orders and use of other methods of influence (such as rewards and punishments) by a formal organization manager over his or her subordinates.

In order to approach more systematically the idea that we are an important part of our own leadership, a simple preliminary framework is useful (a more comprehensive and systematic view of human behavior will be presented later). This framework is what might be referred to as the *reinforcement theory* or *behavior modification view*.[2] It recognizes the importance of events or stimuli that come before and influence behavior (such as giving orders or setting goals), and consequences that are received after the behavior takes place (such as rewards and punishments). The point to recognize, given this framework, is that we do use these same forces on ourselves, though we may not recognize them, or deliberately choose to ignore them. A person who sets goals for personal achievement and who experiences a feeling of exhilaration and self-approval for obtaining them, or a feeling of guilt or self-criticism for not achieving them, is engaging in self-leadership.

A pictorial representation of different sources of leadership follows (see Figure 1-1). It depicts leadership as ranging from an entirely external influence process, at one extreme, to a self-imposed process at the other. This latter focus is the primary topic of this book. In between these two extremes, leadership influence consists of different combinations of external influence and self-influence. When a goal is jointly set by a manager and a subordinate, a participative leadership process is at work.

At this point we are ready to take the next step of our journey; that is, the journey into ourselves toward the realization that we do lead ourselves.

WE ALL LEAD OURSELVES

Even in the most highly controlled situations, we influence our behavior in various ways. If you have a boss who gives you very detailed orders and frequently checks your progress (and probably is not too shy to let you know what you're doing wrong), you still possess a great deal of discretion. The method or order in which you complete tasks, for example, is left to you. What you think about while you work is also up to you. If you choose to set a higher or lower personal goal for yourself than what your boss expects, that too is up to you. You can feel good about your progress or be tough on yourself for even the smallest of mistakes if you choose.

The point is that you are your own leader much of the time. Even if you are faced with very influential external leaders, they are not likely to be staring over your back every minute. In their absence, who is in charge? You, of course. Even if they are present, they cannot look into your mind. In fact, we are our own ultimate leaders. We are capable of negating anything we hear externally and substituting our own internal communication. (Example: From boss: "You're loafing, and what little work you *are* doing is poor quality." To self: "Everyone around here knows I'm the best worker in our department—obviously, the boss is being an unreasonable S.O.B. today.")

Furthermore, what we do with our lives, including where we work and who we work for, is largely left to us. If we need more training to obtain the kind of job we really want, it's up to us to lead ourselves to make the kinds of sacrifices necessary to achieve our ends. I'm not trying to say that it's an easy process. In fact, to lead

Figure 1-1 Sources of Leadership

ourselves to do what we really want is difficult, but it can be done if we know how to go about it.

We all lead ourselves. This is not to say that we are all effective self-leaders. On the contrary, we all have weaknesses in our self-leadership process. In some people the process is very dysfunctional. Many lead themselves into the wrong line of work and into the wrong job; even more lead themselves into unhappiness and discontentment with their lives. Perhaps the saddest of all are those who give up much of their own self-leadership potential to others and are led into equally negative conditions. The point is that you are your own leader, and just like any leader you can be a good one or a bad one. In the pages that follow an attempt will be made to help you understand your own self-leadership patterns and how to improve them. The ideas you choose to adopt for yourself, however, are up to you. After all, you are your own leader.

SELF-LEADERSHIP

Building on the definition of leadership presented earlier in this chapter, self-leadership can be stated as "the process of influencing oneself." This definition is, of course, very general and does not provide the detail necessary to gain a better understanding of or a more effective execution of the process. It does point out, though, the global target at which this book is focused—the process that we experience in influencing ourselves. The primary elements of this process will be presented and discussed throughout the remainder of the book. First, however, an attempt will be made to summarize, in a general sense, the primary ingredients of self-leadership.

The concept of self-leadership is derived primarily from research and theory in two areas of psychology. The first, *social learning theory*,[3] recognizes the adoption and change of human behavior as a complex process with many parts. It recognizes that we influence as well as are influenced by the world we live in (more on this idea in Chapter 2). Importance is also placed on the capacity of a person to manage or control himself—particularly when faced with difficult yet important tasks (this viewpoint serves as the primary basis for Chapter 3). Social learning theory also recognizes the human ability to learn and experience tasks or events through vicarious and symbolic mechanisms (which points out the importance of our ability to learn by observing others and to use our imagination). Chapter 5 will address these ideas more fully. Finally, it stresses the importance of our perceptions of our own effectiveness or potential to be effective (more of this in Chapter 8).

The second important area of knowledge for this book can be described as *intrinsic motivation theory* (and even more specifically as *cognitive evaluation theory*).[4] This viewpoint emphasizes the importance of the "natural" rewards that we enjoy from doing activities or tasks that we like. The ideas included in the writings on intrinsic motivation point out the potential to harness the motivational forces available in doing things that we can really enjoy (Chapter 4 will address these ideas).

The knowledge included in these two insightful areas concerning human behavior represents the major foundation for this book. Ideas will also be borrowed from other bodies of knowledge, including motivation theory and leadership theory. Overall, this book will recognize the importance of forces that we use to influence ourselves (often without even being aware of them) and the potential for altering our worlds so that they are more motivating to us. The major focus will be on the motivational aspects of self-leadership, and less focus on individual abilities or task requirements. The goal is to develop a framework capable of helping you to motivate yourself to achieve your personal goals. The journey has begun—lead onward.

ENDNOTES

[1]Ralph M. Stogdill, *Handbook of Leadership* (New York: Free Press, 1974); and Bernard M. Bass, *Bass and Stogdill's Handbook of Leadership* (New York: Free Press, 1990).

[2]Fred Luthans and Robert Kreitner, *Organizational Behavior Modification and Beyond* (Glenview, Ill.: Scott, Foresman, 1985. Provides a more detailed discussion of this viewpoint as applied to behavior in organizations.

[3]See Albert Bandura, *Social Learning Theory* (Englewood Cliffs, N.J.: Prentice Hall, 1977); and Albert Bandura, *Social Foundations of Thought and Action: A Social Cognitive Theory* (Englewood Cliffs, N.J.: Prentice Hall, 1986).

[4]See, for example, Edward Deci and Richard Ryan, "The Empirical Exploration of Intrinsic Motivational Processes" in L. Berkowitz (ed.), *Advances in Experimental Social Psychology*, vol. 13, 1980; and Edward Deci, *Intrinsic Motivation* (New York: Plenum, 1975).

2

Mapping the Route
or
We Do Choose

The wisest of insights that can be gained by any man or woman is the realization that our world is not so much what it is but what we choose it to be.

Statement made by a wise individual—
or if it wasn't, it should have been.

A number of years ago I worked as a retail clothing salesperson during a Christmas holiday break from college. One particularly hectic day I observed a woman, amidst a mob of customers, looking through piles of casual slacks. She was obviously very frustrated, and grumbled as she worked her way through the piles. I had been straightening the pants between helping what seemed to be an endless onslaught of customers and I noted that the woman's method of searching was, much to my dismay, essentially to destroy slacks by throwing pants on the floor or stuff them in other piles as she continued her search. Finally, she turned to a customer nearby and commented, in obvious displeasure, that the slacks were in a totally disorganized mess, and she could not find the size she needed. At this point, being a bit tired and irritable myself and having watched her undo a substantial amount of my work, I turned to her and said, "You know why they're a mess, don't you?" She looked at me, obviously surprised, and thought a few moments and said, "I suppose because of impatient, pushy ladies like me."

Many of us practice the same kind of behavior throughout our lives, and, unfortunately, it often concerns considerably more important matters. For example, the way we behave toward others will largely determine the way they behave toward us. We can alienate people and then complain (just as the woman did in the clothing store) about the mess our relationship is in. It is important to realize, though, that we do impact on our world just as it impacts on us. We change the world just by being alive. We breathe the air, we take up space, we consume limited food resources, and so on.

We may even bring out the hostility in others just by being alive. I recall quite vividly an experience that I had when I was about 16 years old. I was walking down a long hall in my high school, thinking of nothing in particular, when I heard a very exasperated sigh behind me. I turned around to receive a lethal look from a girl in my class, and to hear the words "would you get out of my way?" snapped at me. It turned out that this young lady wanted to walk faster than I and had tried several times (unsuccessfully, given the crowd of students in the hall) to pass me. By the time I realized that she was competing for my physical space, my existence as a living being had already made her very angry. Most of us could probably offer similar examples that were experienced in crowded restaurants or traffic jams.

Of course, we have little control over the impact we have on the world in cases such as these. What is of greater importance is the behavior that we freely choose to practice. What we choose to do with our lives and how we go about accomplishing our chosen ends will substantially shape the relevant world in which we live. In order to appreciate the importance of this idea, several issues need to be addressed. The first concerns the substantial impact that the world has on us.

THOSE EXTERNAL FACTORS

The world we live in *does* influence what we do with ourselves on a day-to-day basis and can largely shape our ultimate destiny in life. The reinforcement theory view (mentioned in Chapter 1), for example, points out the importance of events that occur before and after our behavior. Considerable evidence has been gathered from many different organizations that reveals the important impact that being rewarded has on chosen actions.[1] In fact, one author has gone so far as to write "On the Folly of Rewarding A, While Hoping for B,"[2] suggesting that what we are rewarded for is the type of behavior that we are likely to use even if some other behavior is more desirable. The point is that we do respond to what we experience and especially to what we receive for our efforts.

Being rewarded for what we do can influence what we choose to do in the future. The reason for this is that rewards provide us with both information concerning what leads to positive or negative results and incentives to do what is rewarded. We are more likely to do in the future those things that we anticipate will lead to desirable results and not do those things we expect to lead to negative results. This logic is, of course, very simple and widely supported by research.

We are faced with many influences in our daily living. Laws place limits on our choices, as do rules that we must follow in order to function in organizations of which we are part. If we violate these limits, negative results are likely to follow, such as traffic tickets, dismissal from our jobs, and so on. The intention of this book is not to suggest that external influences such as these are not important; rather, it is to emphasize the important role we play in determining the external influences that will be relevant to us. Also, it is to emphasize the importance of influences that we place on ourselves directly. The world does impact on our lives, but we are in no way helpless pawns.

THOSE PERSONAL FACTORS

Each of us is unique. We all possess certain qualities, ways of thinking, and so forth that help determine how we see the world and what we do with our lives. In order to understand fully our own self-leadership practices, we must recognize the importance of what we are and how we think about things. This book is particularly concerned with our personal differences in terms of the actions we choose. Rather than dealing with abstract concepts such as "attitudes" or "values," a more workable approach is to deal with individual behaviors.

A broad view of the concept of "behavior" is needed to understand self-leadership. Behavior is viewed as taking place at both an observable physical and unobservable mental level. In fact, the events that come before behavior and the results of behavior take place at both a physical and a mental level. Thus, complex chains of behavioral influence take place. This idea is represented pictorially in Figure 2-1. For example, imagine a person who thinks about the joys of trout fishing and decides to skip work that day, but later feels guilty. This example includes a mental event (thinking about fishing) that comes before and influences an actual physical behavior (skipping work). The physical behavior is followed by a mental result (guilt) which is likely to discourage similar behavior in the future.

The way we practice self-leadership is affected by both our unique tendencies in terms of thinking patterns as well as physical action. We can lead ourselves to desired accomplishments by combining these two levels of influence.

To illustrate these ideas further, let me use a TV commercial as an example. Bruce Jenner, a decathlon gold medal winner in the 1976 Olympic games, made the statement in a cereal commercial, "Pour on the training and what do you get?—A gold medal." One might conclude from this statement that Bruce Jenner's motivation for training centered on the Olympic gold medal. My argument would be, "Pour on the training and what do you get?"—Physical pain and exhaustion, blisters, excessive perspiration, and several other consequences that most would view as undesirable. The

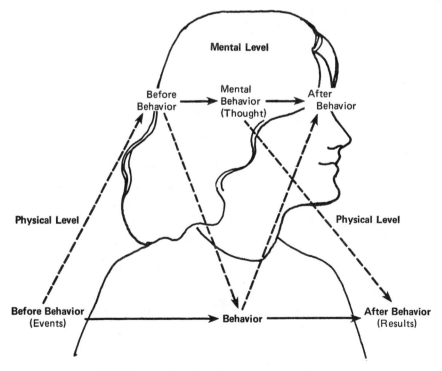

FIGURE 2-1. Mental and Physical Levels of Influence

gold medal is, of course, a worthy pursuit, but a great deal of self-leadership is necessary to carry a person through the sacrifice necessary to reach that final destination.

To maintain the motivation necessary, both physical and mental forces are involved. For example, Bruce Jenner could compete in smaller meets and win awards and recognition on the way to the "gold." He could also picture mentally the moment of victory—standing on the award dais, receiving the gold medal—and later doing Wheaties commercials if he chose to do so. By taking actions (both mental and physical) such as these, the necessary level of motivation can be maintained to complete the difficult training.

The example mentioned above highlights the importance of achieving the level of motivation needed to make difficult sacrifices. This type of self-leadership will be discussed more fully in the next chapter. Self-leadership can also capitalize on the attractiveness of doing things that we like to do (for Bruce Jenner it might be the natural enjoyment of activities such as pole vaulting). This aspect of self-leadership will be dealt with in a later chapter. First, however, this chapter will deal with the mutual influence between persons, their behavior, and their world—and especially, the importance of the choices we make.

WE DO CHOOSE

We as persons, our behavior, and the world we live in are all closely related. Each of these factors places important influences on the others.

For example, our behavior helps to determine what we will be faced with in our world. If our actions generally contribute to the well-being of those we come in contact with, positive forces for a more favorable, relevant world have been put into motion. By taking such actions we can help to ensure the personal security and happiness of others and also increase the likelihood of their being supportive of us. On the other hand, if our actions are strictly for our own benefit, at the cost of others, we may get what we want in the short run but in doing so create a hostile world in which we must live in the longer run. Ebenezer Scrooge creates for himself this sort of hostile world in Charles Dickens's *A Christmas Carol*.

On the other hand, the influence the world has on our behavior is also very important, as was noted earlier in this chapter. Thus, our behavior and our world influence one another. Indeed, Scrooge takes actions that largely create a hostile world for himself—which likely brings out more hostility in Scrooge. A vicious cycle of influence is set into motion which eventually requires the appearance of frightening ghosts so that Scrooge's own behavior breaks the cycle.

A final factor that needs to be included to complete the influence picture is ourselves. Since this book is concerned with behavior as a workable focus for improving our own self-leadership, a useful way of viewing ourselves is in terms of behavioral predispositions. That is, the concern is not with elusive ideas like "good attitudes" or "bad attitudes," but instead—what are our behavioral tendencies (both physical and mental). This viewpoint is represented by questions such as, "How do we tend to react to certain types of situations?" "How do we think about problems?" and so forth. Such tendencies will influence how we behave and how we view the world (the world is probably more a product of the way we see it than what it really is in any concrete sense). Also, our behavioral tendencies or predispositions are greatly influenced by what we experience, such as praise from our fellow humans for certain types of behaviors. They are also influenced by past behaviors. Most of us, for example, tend to develop habits and patterns in our conduct. In addition, it has been suggested that if we change our behaviors, a change in us as persons (attitude) will follow.[3]

The mutual influence between each of these factors is represented pictorially in Figure 2-2. The illustration suggests that we as persons, our world, and our behavior cannot be fully understood separately. Instead, each factor continually influences and is influenced by the other. We should not expect to have circumstances work out to our optimum liking just because we behave in a favorable way. There are other factors involved besides the actions we take. At the same time, we do exercise choices that can have a major impact on what we experience and thus increase our chances for more frequent desirable outcomes.

The choices we make concerning all three parts of the total influence picture are important. First, the world includes potential influences that will not affect us unless we allow them to do so. We do not feel the effects of cold weather unless we leave our dwelling and expose ourselves to the cold. Also, you are not affected by this book unless you choose to read it—it is only a potential influence that is dependent on your choice to pick up a copy and make the effort and take the time to read the words it contains.

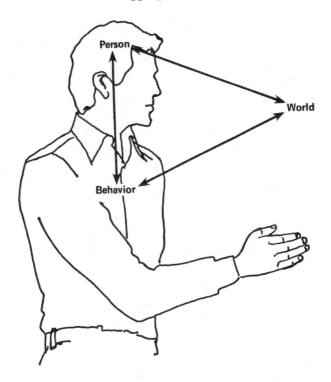

FIGURE 2-2. The Three Factors of the Influence Picture

We also choose the actions we take that in turn influence the world. For me, the ideas I had on self-leadership were only a potential influence for the world until I took the time and made the effort to write this book. If my choosing to write this book helps others to become more effective and contented, then my world is that much improved.

We can also have a choice in how we think about what we experience. For example, we can decide to take an optimistic view of the world, even though many others take a pessimistic one. In doing so we have really accomplished two things. First, our world is going to look more positive to us and as a result will be a more enjoyable place to live. Second, as a result of choosing to take an optimistic view of things we may respond more to the opportunities of life rather than its constraints. Thus, to the extent that we can choose what we are as a person (or, at least, the way we practice thinking about things) we can influence what the world is to us and how we behave toward it.

The point is, even though we function within a complex system of influence, involving ourselves, our behavior, and our world, we do possess a great deal of choice concerning what we experience and what we accomplish with our lives. We are, of course, subject to constraints. These include limitations in our situations (for example, because of the earth's gravity we cannot fly without the aid of equipment of some kind) and the roles in which we find ourselves (such as parents, bosses, citizens). This, however, is no reason to feel helpless. Even when faced with the most difficult situations we do lead ourselves by the choices we make.

To illustrate the importance of choice, let's look at an example involving a rather troubling situation. Imagine that you are the head of a group. The group could be a department in a company, a community group, or whatever else might seem relevant to you. In this group you are faced with a troubling individual. This person always complains at the smallest hint of being slighted in any way. In order to stop these annoying occasions, you have found yourself giving in to his wishes much as a parent might to a whining child. This may involve giving him special privileges that others do not have, or doing things his way even if his way makes things difficult for everyone else. Over time you have fallen into a pattern without recognizing it until it finally becomes a nearly intolerable situation. What can you do?

The solution to the problem is simple—the value of presenting it is in illustrating the issue at hand. You simply choose to stop giving in to the complainer. This may lead to rather annoying experiences at first, but gradually the situation (your world) is likely to improve. In the present pattern you are rewarding this person for complaining, and thereby encouraging the situation to continue and even worsen. You are also being rewarded yourself by eliminating the complaining each time it occurs. Thus, until the choice is made to break the pattern and lead yourself out of the situation, your rewarding behavior is likely to increase, which will make the situation continually worse.

To cope with the immediate negative effects of excessive complaining when you stop giving in, you need to motivate yourself to stand firm. This could be done through methods such as mental support (example: thinking to yourself thoughts such as, "I'm not giving in this time, buster. I know I can stand firm and things are going to improve around here.") or by removing yourself temporarily from the presence of the complainer.

Specific approaches that can be used to lead yourself to do what you set out to do are discussed in the following chapters. The lesson at hand is that we do choose. We do not live in a vacuum that is free from all external forces. But then, would life be very interesting if we did? We are faced with challenges, obstacles, and many difficult situations. All this makes effective self-leadership that much more important and rewarding. We are self-leaders—why not be the best ones we can be? Travel onward and see if you can lead yourself to this end.

ENDNOTES

[1] See, for example, W. Clay Hamner and Ellen P. Hamner, "Behavior Modification on the Bottom Line," *Organizational Dynamics* (Spring 1976), 3–21.

[2] Steven Kerr, "On the Folly of Rewarding A, While Hoping for B," *Academy of Management Journal*, 18 (1975), 769–783.

[3] Arnold P. Goldstein and Melvin Sorcher, *Changing Supervisor Behavior* (New York: Pergamon Press, 1977).

3

Rough Road, Detours, and Roadblocks

or

Leading Ourselves to Do Necessary but Unattractive Tasks

"I can't face another—no, not today," she groaned to herself as she looked at her new formidable challenger.

"You must," she heard from a voice somewhere in the deep recesses of her mind. Only moments before she had overcome what she thought to be her last adversary of the day and had risen to start the journey she had longed for—only to be challenged again. Looking cautiously at the massive features of the beast, she sighed deeply in dismay. But then a strategy came to her and her determination returned. She reached swiftly, but with great control, for her weaponry. Flipping the appropriate switches on the dark rectangle before her, she swung it open. The beast seemed almost to shrink from the sound alone. Then she reached efficiently, coolly, for the mechanism with the illuminated dial and the powerful lance that she knew together could overcome the beast...she braced herself...then, without warning, she was upon it.

Some hours later she backed away wearily, victoriously, from her defeated, now harmless-looking, prey. She had won again but wondered how much longer she could endure such battles. She sighed, stretching and rolling her shoulders, while momentarily closing her eyes. Then slowly, the finished report before her, she returned her calculator and pen to her briefcase and rose for her journey to the suburbs.

Let's face it—it's not always easy to do the things that we know we should. Often the sacrifices and effort necessary to reach our desired destinies and to become fulfilled as people present formidable barriers. So how do we lead ourselves over the rough roads of our life's journey? How do we motivate ourselves to "hang in there" when everything seems to be saying, "Give up you fool—you can't do it"?

Our inner nature might be compared to a constant battle between opposing forces. A part of us seems to say, "Give up; take the easy way out; it's just too difficult; don't even try." Another part of us seems to say, "I do want my life to count for something; I want to become all that I am capable of becoming." So how do we get ourselves to take action and do the things that we believe we should do? How do we get ourselves to face life's hardships and lead ourselves to our own personal victory, to our own chosen destiny? Indeed, in many ways we experience the inner conflict of a Dr. Jekyll and Mr. Hyde. How do we lead ourselves to win the battle where Dr. Jekyll lost?

This chapter is about leading ourselves to do unattractive but necessary tasks. It's about leading ourselves to face the challenges, make the sacrifices, and take the actions that we need to in order to achieve what we choose for ourselves. It will suggest several specific strategies that we can use to manage our own behavior. These strategies are especially suited for motivating and leading ourselves in the face of difficult and, at least in the short run, unappealing but necessary tasks (undesirable desirables).

Take a few moments to assess some of your own self-leadership tendencies. Respond to the following self-assessment questionnaire by circling the number corresponding to the description (e.g., describes me very well, describes me well, and so on) that you believe best reflects your position regarding each of the statements included. Some of the statements (1 through 18) may seem a bit redundant. Try not to let this bother you. Respond to each statement even though some of them may seem quite similar. Score your responses according to the directions provided. You may want to indicate your responses and calculate your score on a separate sheet of paper. That way you can reuse the questionnaires and exercises, included in this book, at a later date without being biased by your earlier responses.

Self-Leadership Questionnaire 1 (SLQ1)
Self-Assessment Questionnaire for Dealing with
Unattractive but Necessary Tasks

		Describes Me Very Well	Describes Me Well	Describes Me Somewhat	Does Not Describe Me Very Well	Does Not Describe Me At All
1.	I try to keep track of how well I'm doing while I work	5	4	3	2	1
2.	I often use reminders to help me remember things I need to do	5	4	3	2	1
3.	I like to work toward specific goals I set for myself	5	4	3	2	1
4.	After I perform well on an activity, I feel good about myself	5	4	3	2	1
5.	I tend to get down on myself when I have performed poorly	5	4	3	2	1
6.	I often practice important tasks before I actually do them	5	4	3	2	1
7.	I usually am aware of how I am performing on an activity	5	4	3	2	1
8.	I try to arrange my work area in a way that helps me positively focus my attention on my work	5	4	3	2	1
9.	I establish personal goals for myself	5	4	3	2	1
10.	When I have successfully completed a task, I often reward myself with something I like	5	4	3	2	1

Table (cont.)

		Describes Me Very Well	Describes Me Well	Describes Me Somewhat	Does Not Describe Me Very Well	Does Not Describe Me At All
11.	I tend to be tough on myself when I have not done well on a task	5	4	3	2	1
12.	I like to go over an important activity before I actually perform it	5	4	3	2	1
13.	I keep track of my progress on projects I'm working on	5	4	3	2	1
14.	I try to surround myself with objects and people that bring out my desirable behaviors	5	4	3	2	1
15.	I like to set task goals for my performance	5	4	3	2	1
16.	When I do an assignment especially well, I like to treat myself to something or an activity I enjoy	5	4	3	2	1
17.	I am often critical of myself concerning my failures	5	4	3	2	1
18.	I often rehearse my plan for dealing with a challenge before I actually face the challenge	5	4	3	2	1

Directions for scoring. Total your responses for A through F, X, and XX (listed on the following page) by adding the numbers you circled for each of the statements as indicated in parentheses.

A. Self observation (add numbers circled for statements 1, 7, and 13) _____

B. Cueing strategies (add numbers circled for statements 2, 8, and 14) _____

C. Seff-goal-setting (add numbers circled for statements 3, 9, and 15 _____

D. Self-reward (add numbers circled for statements 4, 10, and 16) _____

E. Self-punishment (add numbers circled for statements 5, 11, and 17) _____

F. Practice (add numbers circled for statements 6, 12, and 18) _____

X Total score, including self-punishment (add scores for A through F) _____

XX Total score, not including self-punishment (add scores for A through F, except E) _____

Interpreting Your Score

Your score for A through F suggests your current self-leadership tendencies concerning six self-leadership strategies that will be addressed in this chapter. Your score for each of these strategies could range from 3 (a total absence of the strategy in your current behavior) to 15 (a very high level of the strategy in your current behavior).

Your score on A through F can be interpreted as follows:

1. A score of 3 or 4 indicates a *very low* level of the strategy

2. A score of 5 to 7 indicates a *low* level of the strategy

3. A score of 8 to 10 indicates a *moderate* level of the strategy

4. A score of 11 to 13 indicates a *high* level of the strategy

5. A score of 14 or 15 indicates a *very high* level of the strategy

Evidence indicates that the use of each of these strategies tends to be related to higher performance, with the exception of self-punishment (E). Therefore, a high score on A, B, C, D, and F reflects a high level of self-leadership, which is likely to enhance your performance. A high score on E, on the other hand, reflects a high level of self-punishment, which may actually detract from your performance. Each of these strategies is discussed in more detail throughout the remainder of the chapter.

Your score on X indicates your overall use of all of the above self-leadership strategies, including self-punishment. Your score could range from a low of 18 to a high of 90. Your score on X is not easy to interpret since it includes self-punishment, which may actually detract from performance. Your score on XX, on the other hand, reflects your score on only the five self-leadership strategies which, in general, are positively related to performance (your score could range from 15 to 75). Your score on XX can be interpreted as follows:

1. A score of 15 to 22 indicates a *very low* overall level of the strategies

2. A score of 23 to 37 indicates a *low* overall level of the strategies

3. A score of 38 to 52 indicates a *moderate* overall level of the strategies

4. A score of 53 to 67 indicates a *high* overall level of the strategies

5. A score of 68 to 75 indicates a *very high* overall level of the strategies

In general, a high score on XX suggests that you already possess some positive self-leadership tendencies. Regardless of what your score is, this chapter is designed to help you implement and improve upon several self-leadership techniques that are available. If you scored high on the questionnaire, this indicates that you believe you are exercising these self-influence methods. Whether you are actually using them or using them *effectively* is, of course, a different matter.

The field of psychology has recently provided some interesting discoveries regarding means we use to control our own behavior. The area of thought that has come to be called *self-control* or *self-management* is especially insightful.[1] A number of useful techniques for getting ourselves to do the "undesirable desirables" are suggested by the work in this area.[2] Some of the strategies that are available are addressed in the questionnaire you have just completed and will be discussed in the remainder of the chapter. These strategies can be classified under two general approaches: strategies that alter the world, and the way it impacts on us, in a beneficial way; and strategies that we directly impose upon ourselves to influence our own behavior. By reading the remainder of this chapter you will gain insight on how to implement these strategies more fully and effectively into your own self-leadership. Guidelines will be offered, including checklists that summarize the primary steps involved as well as exercises to help you get started in practicing systematic self-leadership.

WORLD-ALTERING STRATEGIES

We do possess the ability to make alterations in our immediate worlds that will help us to behave in desirable ways. Many of these alterations are very simple yet capable of really making a difference in our actions. Three different strategies will be offered here.

Reminders and Attention Focusers

What's this piece of paper with a big letter A on it doing on your office door? It's to remind me to buy my wife flowers for our anniversary. I forgot last year and if I forget again she'll skin me alive.

This first strategy involves using physical objects to remind us of, or to focus our attention on, things we need to do. Probably the most well-known traditional example of this strategy is tying a string around one of our fingers to remind us of something. Admittedly, if we used this method today we would probably be met with amusement and embarrassing comments from those we associate with. There are many other methods available, though, that are in a similar vein and that offer practical benefits.

One simple strategy that has been emphasized for improving the effectiveness of our management of time is to make a list of our pending tasks.[3] At the beginning of a workday, for example, simply sit down and make a list of all the important things that need to be done during the day. If possible, priorize the list and then keep it handy throughout the day. The list not only serves as a reminder and guide but can also provide the basis for a feeling of personal accomplishment and reward as items are crossed off the list.

Many additional techniques are available. For example, if we have a top priority project that needs to be done, we can place it in the center of our work space. Whenever we return to our work area we have a powerful reminder of our most pressing task. The important point is that we can use physical cues to focus our efforts. The challenge is to find those reminders and attention focusers that work best for us and to use them.

Removing Negative Cues

Every time we go to that restaurant I am overcome by the dessert display. For the good of my diet can't we go somewhere else for lunch today?

If we wish to eliminate our behaviors that we don't like, one strategy is to eliminate cues that might lead to these behaviors. If we wish to cut down on our consumption of sweets, for example, we can remove the candy dish from the coffee table. Similarly, if we are disturbed about excessive time spent watching television, we can move the TV set to another less frequently used room.

The point is that we are surrounded by physical cues that tend to encourage certain behaviors. If we can identify the things in our world that encourage our undesired behaviors, we can either remove or alter them. In addition, we can remove ourselves from their presence. If we need to get some work done, for example, we are well advised to leave the TV room or game room (with all their powerful cues) and go to a study room. In fact we can design the layout of the rooms in our homes with healthy, constructive living kept in mind. Similarly, we can design our work space to eliminate cues to destructive, unproductive behavior.

Increasing Positive Cues

I think placing the safety record displays around the plant has really had positive results. It keeps our workers thinking about safety and our accident record has improved.

Another strategy involves increasing the cues that tend to lead to our positive behaviors. If we decide that we would like to become more knowledgeable on a particular subject but find that we never take the time to read much on that subject, what can we do? We can set up cues that will encourage our reading. We could, for example, place appropriate books on a table next to our favorite comfortable chair. We may then be faced with a choice between cues for reading and some other activity like watching television (if we have not removed the TV set), but at least we are more aware of the choice.

We can also arrange cues that impact on very important matters—such as what kind of persons we can become. The organization we work in, for example, contains many important cues for both desired and undesired behavior. If our workplace contains more negative cues than positive cues, we can try to alter the cues available, or if this is not possible, perhaps it's time to make a job change.

The people you work with serve as very powerful cues—are their values consistent with yours? Over time the people we work with are likely to influence what we become. If we know ourselves, what we are striving toward, and what we believe in, it is important to surround ourselves with the right people. We are likely to select role models from among our associates. Do your present role models display behaviors that are consistent with the achievement of what you have chosen for yourself? If we work with people whom we view as using unethical means to achieve their ends, we are exposing ourselves to undesirable cues. On the other hand, we can choose to associate with persons who act in consistent ways with our values and who successfully achieve the worthwhile ends we desire. By choosing such an organization and consequently the people who work there, we establish positive cues for our behavior.

The following checklist is provided to summarize the major steps for exercising self-leadership through the use of world-altering (cues) strategies. The primary objective of the strategies is stated next to the first checkbox and a list of the primary steps involved follows. (Note: This general format will be adopted in all the checklists throughout this book.)

Also, extra checkboxes are included at the bottom of each of the checklists provided in this book so that you can think of additional steps you believe would be helpful to you. In addition, an exercise is provided to help you get started in applying these techniques.

Checklist for Using Cues

☐ Use cues to help you exercise self-leadership

    ☐ Use physical cues to remind you of your important tasks—for example, make lists to guide your daily activities

    ☐ Establish cues to focus your attention on important behaviors and tasks—for example, place helpful signs around your work area that focus your thinking in desired ways

    ☐ Identify and reduce or eliminate negative cues in your work environment—for example, remove objects you find distracting

    ☐ Identify and increase positive cues in your work environment

    ☐ Wherever possible, associate and surround yourself with people who cue your desirable behavior

    ☐

Cues Exercise

Study how cues affect your behavior. (Make notes.)

1. How do you use reminders and attention focusers?

2. What are some ways you could improve on your use of reminders and attention focusers?

3. List some negative cues in your work environment that are encouraging your undesirable behaviors.

4. How might you reduce or eliminate these negative cues?

5. List some positive cues in your work environment that are encouraging your desirable behaviors.

6. How might you increase these positive cues?

SELF-IMPOSED STRATEGIES

In addition to creating or altering cues in our world to influence our own behavior, we can directly exercise control over ourselves. The cement that lays the foundation for this self-imposed control is the information we possess about ourselves—or, in other words, *self-awareness*. By observing our own behavior and its causes (for example, why we behave in desirable or undesirable ways) we are provided with the necessary information to manage ourselves effectively. Thus, the first self-imposed strategy is *self-observation*.

Self-Observation

"That is the third time I've lost my temper and criticized someone today, and I've done it several other times this week. I wonder what's wrong and why I'm behaving like such an ogre."

Self-observation involves determining when, why, and under what conditions we use certain behaviors. For example, if we feel we are not accomplishing enough each day in our work because of wasted time, we can study the distractions we experience. Are we spending too much time engaged in informal conversations? By observing the amount of informal conversing we participate in and the conditions that exist at the time, we can learn more about this behavior. If five hours are spent chatting during the eight-hour workday, we probably have a problem. Furthermore, if most of these conversations begin during a visit to the office water cooler, we have useful information to help us cut down on the behavior (we need to cut down on our trips to the water cooler).

Additional power can be added to this strategy if we physically record our self-observations. A handy pen and a 3″ × 5″ card may be all we need to make brief notes that can be examined in detail later on.

Self-observation can provide the foundation for managing our behavior. Several other distinct strategies build on this foundation. It is important to remember that we already use these strategies in our daily living; the problem is that we often use them unknowingly and ineffectively.

A checklist summarizing the major steps for practicing self-observation follows. Also, an exercise is included to help you get started using self-observation.

Checklist for Self-Observation

☐ Use self-observation as a basis for self-leadership

   ☐ Identify your behaviors that you feel are especially important that you would like either to increase or reduce

   ☐ Keep a record of the frequency and duration of these important behaviors

   ☐ Note the conditions that exist when these behaviors are displayed

   ☐ Identify other important factors concerning these behaviors— for example, the time of day or week they tend to occur, or who is present at the time

   ☐ Whenever possible, keep a written record of your self-observations, but try to keep the process simple enough so that you will not be discouraged from using it

   ☐

Self-Observation Exercise

Develop your self-awareness. Intentionally observe yourself for the next week. Make notes about behaviors that you see as desirable and undesirable. Include the frequency and duration with which they occur, when they occur, and why you think they occur (identified reasons for your behaviors should include both external world influences and directly self-imposed influences). Develop your own self-observation system for future use.

BEHAVIOR	FREQUENCY AND DURATION	WHEN (DAY/TIME)	WHY (EXTERNAL AND INTERNAL INFLUENCES)

Self-Goal-Setting

"I don't know where I'm going, but I'm getting there awfully fast," gasped the man as he scurried on past.

It is futile to exert effort with no direction. One way we can provide ourselves direction in our self-leadership is through the use of personal goals. What we strive toward in terms of our long-term life achievements as well as on a daily basis influences our behavior. Often we are not clear on what our goals really are. We may wish to achieve a position of importance and influence in life, for example, but we do not settle on how we will go about obtaining the position, or even what the position is. The systematic, thought-out, intentional setting of personal goals can positively influence our behavior.

Self-set goals need to address our long-range pursuits and our short-run objectives along the way. If we decide on a long-range goal of becoming a lawyer, we need to accomplish many shorter-range goals such as acceptance into law school and passing courses once we are admitted. Our immediate behavior in turn should be pointing at specific short-term, meaningful goals such as reading a law journal (or a few pages in a journal) or completing a law brief (or a portion of a brief). The shorter-range goals should be consistent with the longer-range goals for maximum effectiveness. We must first engage in the necessary self-analysis to understand what we want out of life before we can set the goals that must be reached in order to achieve these ends. This takes effort. Also, our goals are likely to change over time. It is important, though, that we try to have current goals for our immediate efforts.

Generally, goals are more effective for managing our immediate behavior if they are specific and challenging, yet achievable. If we set unreasonable goals that we cannot realistically achieve, we are likely to do more harm than good. Realistic achievable goals, on the other hand, can be very satisfying when we achieve them.

If we understand what we value in life and what we want to accomplish, then we can set specific achievable goals (such as reading one hour each day on a given subject or attending a lecture to improve our skills in a given area). It is often helpful to record in writing both our long-term and immediate goals and then modify them as necessary. We spend a great deal of time doing things with our lives. A little effort expended on setting self-goals can help us to have purpose and direction so that we don't waste our efforts.

> The man stopped abruptly with surprise and in a panting voice said, "Why, I'm right where I started. I've gotten nowhere."

The checklist for using self-goal-setting follows. Also, an exercise that includes a guide for conducting an all-important self-analysis and an opportunity to establish long- and short-term goals is provided.

Self-Goal-Setting Exercise

Answer the following questions to help you set long-term and short-term goals.

Long-term goals

1. What do I value most in life (e.g., prestige, wealth, acceptance of others, family relations)?

2. a. What would I most like to accomplish during my lifetime? (Note: An interesting way to approach this question is to write your ideal obituary including all that you would like to have accomplished before you die.)

   b. Develop a list of long-term goals.

Goals for developing abilities to reach long-term goals

3. What are my primary strengths and weaknesses that are related to what I would like to accomplish?

4. What do I need to do to prepare myself to accomplish my long-term goals (e.g., education, skills that need developing)?

Short-term goals

5. What do I need to do now (today, this week) to progress toward my long-term goals (e.g., read a book, complete a task)? Develop a list of short-term goals and update it as needed.

Checklist for Self-Goal-Setting

☐ Use self-goal-setting to establish direction for your efforts

    ☐ Conduct a self-analysis to help you establish long-term goals (see the self-goal-setting exercise)

    ☐ Establish long-run goals for your life and career—for example, what do you want to be doing and where do you want to be 10 years from now? 20 years?

    ☐ Establish short-run goals for your immediate efforts

☐ Keep your goals specific and concrete

☐ Make your goals challenging but reasonable for your own abilities

☐ When feasible, let others know about your goals to provide you with added incentive to achieve them

☐

☐

Self-Reward

After giving the speech she walked as though floating to her chair, sat down slowly, and thought to herself, "Well I'll be darned, I did a hell of a job."

One of the most powerful methods we possess to lead ourselves to new achievements is self-reward. We can positively influence our actions by rewarding ourselves for desirable behavior. Furthermore, we are capable of rewarding ourselves at both a physical and mental level.

At the physical level we can reward ourselves with objects that we desire. In my executive development seminars and college courses, people have revealed numerous ways that they have used things they value to reward themselves. Some of the rewards they have used for completing tasks include ice cream, shopping, watching television, listening to a stereo, and going out to eat. By rewarding themselves with desired items such as these, a positive effect can be exerted on their future work activity. An example is a salesperson who rewards himself/herself with a day off or an expensive dinner after making a big sale.

The important point is that we can reward ourselves with things that we enjoy when we accomplish desired objectives. Many of us do this without realizing it is happening. To increase our own motivation and effectiveness, the challenge is to identify those things we find rewarding and then use them systematically to reward our behavior. By having an exquisite dinner out after we finally talk to that problem employee we've been avoiding, we are providing incentive for ourselves to use similar desired behavior in the future.

We can also reward ourselves at a mental level. We can do this through internal speech and through our imagination. If a salesperson does finally make that big sale, he may be calm on the outside, but if we could listen inside we might hear, "Ya hoo ... I did it ... I'm a genius ... I'm the best ... Ya hoo ..." I often wondered what a professional baseball player is thinking after hitting the game-winning home run in the ninth inning. We all probably engage in self-rewarding internal speech after big successes like these, but why not try to use this powerful method for less momentous occasions? In fact, we could probably significantly improve our own behavior if we purposefully sought out our desirable behaviors and gave ourselves an internal word of praise.

This would be especially useful for those persons who are quick to criticize themselves. We have a choice between focusing on what we've done right and "building ourselves up," or focusing on what we've done wrong and "getting down" on ourselves. The research done in this area indicates that the former strategy is the more effective one. Guilt and self-criticism may have their place in keeping us from engaging in socially and personally undesirable acts, but to rely on these mechanisms and ignore self-praise is a poor way to lead ourselves. Our self-esteem, enthusiasm, and enjoyment in life would likely suffer.

We can also reward ourselves in our imagination. For example, we can journey to our favorite vacation spot in an instant through our imagination. We can close our eyes and see the deep blue waters and the white sand, beaches with seagulls overhead, and feel the warm sun on our face. Or maybe it's the cool air we feel rushing across our face as our skis glide gracefully through the pure white new-fallen snow. Wherever and whatever that place is, we can go there in an instant and we can take the trip as a reward for finally getting that difficult report done or for accomplishing some other task. We might even hang a picture of the place on a wall and keep souvenirs nearby to help us make that mental trip when we choose to make it.

In fact, we can combine the physical and mental levels to exercise a particularly powerful self-reward strategy. We could take short, imaginary trips as we accomplish our tasks throughout the year and then physically enjoy our vacation after the months of hard work. By doing so we are rewarding our short-run and long-run activities. Also, the actual vacation will renew the basis for especially enjoyable imaginary trips when our mind is called on to reproduce the physical setting once we are back at work.

We can also use our imagination to reward ourselves in countless other ways. We can picture the success and esteem we will experience and enjoy when we finally get that promotion we are working toward. Enjoyment of such an image after completion of each difficult task can help us to maintain the motivation we need as we face our labors. Indeed, the mind is capable of being a powerfully motivating tool. If we are to become truly effective self-leaders, we need to master the use of this tool. In doing so we can make the effort we expend seem worthwhile if not truly enjoyable. A checklist to guide your attempts in mastering self-reward follows along with an exercise to help you put these steps into practice.

Self-Reward Exercise

Identify what you find rewarding.

1. What physical objects or events do you find rewarding (e.g., a delicious dinner, an evening out)?

2. What thoughts or images do you find rewarding (e.g., self-praising thoughts, imagination of your favorite vacation spot, thoughts about future career success and prestige)?

3. Identify behaviors that you would like to increase or improve on that require special motivation for you to do them (e.g., reading a technical book, working on a difficult project). Make a list.

4. Try rewarding yourself for working on the activities you have identified in step 3. Use physical and mental rewards. Keep track of your efforts on these behaviors, the rewards you use, and the results and ideas for future improvement (e.g., more effective rewards discovered) stemming from the self-reward process.

BEHAVIOR	*REWARDS USED*	*RESULTS AND IDEAS*

Checklist for Self-Reward

☐ Achieve self-motivation through self-reward.

  ☐ Identify what motivates you—which objects, thoughts, images

  ☐ Identify your behaviors and activities that you believe are especially desirable

  ☐ Reward yourself when you successfully complete an activity or engage in desirable behavior

  ☐ Potential rewards you can use include:

    1. Desired physical objects such as an expensive dinner, a night out on the town, simply a cup of coffee or a snack, or reading a good book
    2. Enjoyable or praising thoughts such as thinking to yourself that you performed well and reminding yourself of future benefits you might receive from continued high performance
    3. Pleasant images such as imagination of your favorite vacation spot

  ☐ Develop the habit of being self-praising and self-rewarding for your accomplishments

  ☐

Self-Punishment

After giving the speech, she dragged herself to her chair, sat down dejectedly, and thought to herself, "I really did a lousy job."

One way that we lead ourselves is through the application of various self-punishments. Unfortunately, it seems that many individuals rely too heavily on this approach. Habitual guilt and self-criticism can impair our motivation and creativity.

Self-punishment operates in much the same way as self-reward in that it focuses on self-applied consequences for our behavior. The difference is that it involves negative rather than positive self-applied results in order to decrease undesired rather than increase desired behavior. A salesperson, for example, might engage in self-punishment after making what he/she thinks was a poor sales presentation. Refusal to play that weekly game of golf or watch the big game on TV and forcing himself/herself instead to work endlessly on the sales presentation is an example of how self-punishment might be carried out at the physical level. At the mental level, negative internal speech (Example: "I really did a lousy job ... I should be ashamed of myself") or images of possible negative results of the behavior (for example, imagining loss of one's job and not being able to afford to pay the bills and support the family) can provide the self-punishments.

Research and writing have generally indicated that self-punishment is not a very effective strategy for controlling our behavior. First of all, if we are applying the punishment to ourselves we can freely avoid it. In other words, if we decide purposefully to use self-punishment to eliminate our undesired behaviors, we are likely to find that we will not use it consistently because it is unpleasant and we can choose to avoid it. On the other hand, those who do use it consistently (often in a habitual manner without even realizing it) are likely to become discouraged and not enjoy their work.

There are times, though, that we do need to work on our negative behaviors—so what can we do? Probably a better strategy would be to try to remove any rewards supporting the problem behavior and apply self-reward when we do things right. Self-observation will be important to accomplish this strategy. For example, imagine that we identify our problem behavior as watching too much television. One thing we might do is allow ourselves to watch only our second or third choice of programs on certain days, thus removing some of the reward of watching. Also, we could keep a record of how much television we are watching and reward ourselves when we substantially decrease our viewing time (for example, an expensive dinner out or even a free night of watching television all we want).

Similar strategies could be used to deal with many of our problem behaviors. Self-punishment may be useful at times such as when we experience guilt after doing something we know is obviously very wrong. To live without a conscience would perhaps be to be inhuman. In most cases, though, we can more constructively deal with our problem behaviors by studying them, removing the rewards that support them, and rewarding related behaviors that are desirable. The goal should be to take constructive action to correct these behaviors and not to demoralize and psychologically paralyze ourselves by dwelling on them.

A checklist for gaining control of your self-punishment patterns follows. Also, an exercise is provided to help you get started in constructively controlling your undesirable behaviors.

Self-Punishment Exercise

Study your self-punishment patterns.

1. What are some of the behaviors that result in your feeling guilty?

2. What are some of the behaviors that result in your feeling critical about yourself?

3. Think about the behaviors that you have identified in step 1 and step 2. Is your guilt and self-criticism constructive or destructive?

4. In the next few days try a different self-leadership strategy for dealing with your undesirable behavior in cases where you think your self-punishment is destructive:

   a. Try to identify and remove rewards that are encouraging your negative behaviors

   b. Try reinforcing related, more desirable behaviors (e.g., rewarding yourself for being calm and dealing rationally with conflicts with others rather than exploding with anger.)

Keep track of your progress.

UNDESIRABLE BEHAVIOR	_STRATEGY USED_	_COMMENTS_

Checklist for Self-Punishment

☐ Control your self-punishment patterns

    ☐ Identify behaviors that you feel guilty about

    ☐ Identify your actions that result in your being self-critical

    ☐ Identify your destructive self-punitive tendencies

    ☐ Work on reducing or eliminating habitual destructive self-punishment patterns

    ☐ Try alternative strategies to self-punishment for dealing with your negative behavior, such as:

        • identifying and removing rewards that support your negative behavior

        • establishing rewards for behaviors that are more desirable than your negative behaviors and that could be substituted for them

    ☐ In general, reserve self-punishment for only your very wrong, seriously negative behaviors.

☐

Practice

"Hey, isn't this the third time you've been out here hitting balls this week?"
"Yes, it is. I'm tired of playing golf in the wrong fairway. I'm going to practice until I get rid of this slice."

One way we can improve our behavior is through practice. By going over activities before we are called on to perform them "when it counts" we can detect problems and make corrections. In doing so we are able to avoid costly errors. For example, suppose we have developed a work plan for our place of employment that we strongly believe will improve profits for the company and working conditions for workers. Also, suppose we have been allowed 15 minutes to propose the plan to a group of executives who will decide whether or not it is adopted. Needless to say, we will want to make those 15 minutes count. Therefore, it is in our own best interest to practice our presentation ahead of time.

We can practice at both a physical level and a mental level. For the situation just discussed, we can verbally practice our presentation in front of a mirror or in front of willing friends, or we can go over the key points we want to make in our minds. An Olympic athlete can take the same approach: He can practice the event repeatedly at a physical level as well as rehearse the event mentally before competing.

Also, practice can be paired with self-rewards to increase motivation and self-confidence. In addition to mentally rehearsing our presentation, for example, we can picture praise from our audience and adoption of the plan. An Olympic athlete could picture winning the gold medal and the benefits that go with such an accomplishment.

Practice can be a powerful strategy to improve our behavior. The challenge is to apply it systematically. In essence we need to practice practicing. The key is to develop the ability to identify the important parts of a given task, to practice them both physically and mentally, and to pair our practices with rewards. The more important the activity, the more important it is to practice. Practice may not make perfect, but it can make better—if we use it.

A checklist to guide your putting practice into practice follows. An exercise is also provided to get you started practicing.

Checklist for Practice

☐ Improve future performance through practice

  ☐ Identify especially important upcoming challenges

  ☐ Note the important components of these future challenges

  ☐ Physically practice these key components—for example, practice an important oral presentation, focusing special effort on the key points to be made

  ☐ Mentally practice key components while thinking about possible improvements in the performance plan

  ☐ Pair your practice with rewards—for example, while mentally going over a future challenge, imagine a positive, rewarding outcome resulting from your actions

  ☐

Practice Exercise

Use physical and mental practice to improve your performance. Make notes.

1. Identify those challenges you believe will be most important for you in the next few weeks.

2. What are the important components/steps involved in dealing with the challenges identified above?

3. Practice your performance plan to deal with these challenges. Practice physically and mentally and pair your practice with rewards. Keep a record of your practices, and possible improvements and ideas identified during them.

BEHAVIOR PRACTICED   *WHEN PRACTICED*   *IDEAS AND POSSIBLE MPROVEMENTS*

Over the past few years I have asked hundreds of participants in my executive development seminars and MBA classes to complete personal improvement projects applying the strategies that are presented in this book. They were simply asked to apply the strategies that seemed most appealing to them to address some aspect of their work or life that they would like to improve on. The following short case (and the ones at the end of the next two chapters) is a composite example based on the experiences of these many managers, executives, MBA students, doctors, technical specialists, and persons in many other career paths.

THE CASE OF THE SALES REP WHO NEGLECTED TO BRING IN NEW CLIENTS

Jack was a district sales representative for AB Company. He was very well thought of by his clients. He serviced his accounts about as well as anyone in the business. Jack developed very good relationships with these clients by continuously looking for new and better ways to provide excellent service. He called on each and every client on a regular basis and asked about their current needs and for inputs concerning suggestions for improving his service to them. Jack generally liked his customers and enjoyed talking and visiting with them.

Despite his strong commitment to service and the high level of satisfaction of his clients, Jack was considered only an average producer in the company. He rarely lost an existing account, but his success in bringing in new clients was very low. He was selling in a growing industry and district sales representatives in his company were increasing their client base at a rate of about 9 percent a year. Jack, on the other hand, was increasing his clients by about 4 percent a year. The zone sales manager had just reviewed Jack's performance with him the day before and made it clear to Jack that his new customer growth was simply inadequate. Jack still felt a little angry as he recounted the conversation in his mind. After all, he did have the lowest rate of lost clients in his region, and a recent survey of his customers revealed a satisfaction level that was among the highest in the company.

Nevertheless, Jack realized that he was going to have to make some changes if he wanted to advance in the company. He was going to have to build his client base at an increased rate. At the same time, he also realized that he simply did not enjoy calling on potentially new clients nearly as much as he did clients that he had gotten to know over the years and in many cases had developed personal friendships with.

To address the problem, Jack reasoned that he had to get a better handle on how he was spending his current time and efforts. He began by keeping a detailed log of his activities for a week (self-observation). He recorded the times that he undertook various tasks, what specifically he did, the purpose of the activity, and how long he spent on it. During this initial self-observation period, Jack made no effort to change his work routine. At the end of the observation period, he discovered some revealing patterns. First he had spent about 47 hours (about 95 percent of his time) either doing routine paper work, attending meetings, or servicing clients. He had spent less than a total of two hours on efforts to communicate with only three potential new clients, all of which came from referrals from existing clients. While he recognized the positive role of the referrals from satisfied customers (and he had received preliminary agreement for a modest sale to one of these referrals), Jack also realized that he was spending much too little time on generating new business.

As a second step, Jack decided to set a goal to increase his time spent on seeking new customers to six hours over the next week and decided that he would further increase the time he spent on this activity by one half hour a week over the next four weeks until he reached a total of eight hours per week (self-goal-setting). After recording this goal on a pad of paper, Jack realized that he felt a bit uneasy about spending that much time on an activity that he did not enjoy very much. Furthermore, he knew his referrals would cover only a small portion of that time and that he would have to spend much of the time proactively seeking new leads and making some cold calls on potential customers. He concluded that he needed to create a way of rewarding himself for reaching his goal. His approach was to take a short coffee break immediately after each solid hour he spent on generating new business (self-reward). He also decided if he met his goal that he would take his wife out to one of their favorite restaurants at the end of the week to celebrate. He also planned to add additional rewards for meeting his increasing goals over the coming weeks.

As an additional strategy, Jack placed a sign on the wall in front of his desk that read "Your best customers will be the one's you haven't even met yet" (cueing strategy). This helped Jack to keep his new goal constantly in mind and helped him to feel positive about the possibility that many of the new clients he would gain could lead to some of his most satisfying relationships in the future. Finally, he spent some time in the office and at home rehearsing (practicing) new approaches for calling on potential new clients. He did this in front of a mirror, with his wife, or with a willing co-worker. Interestingly, he discovered that when he rehearsed with others they often gave him suggestions and tips on how to improve his approach.

Jack's self-leadership efforts proved very successful. Over the next several weeks he increased his goal to ten hours a week spent on generating new business, which he faithfully met. In addition, he increased his generation of new clients to about 14 percent for the year, which was one of the highest levels in the region. He was also pleased to discover that his service to existing clients didn't suffer; he simply spent more time dedicated to the important needs of his customers. His performance review for the next year went very well, and Jack received a substantial pay increase. Over time Jack realized that he was pretty good at generating new business. While he didn't enjoy this activity quite as much as servicing existing clients, he was confident, with the aid of his self-leadership strategies, that he would be able to maintain significant success in this area for years to come.

This chapter has presented several strategies for understanding and improving self-leadership in the face of difficult challenges and activities. Checklists and exercises were provided to help make these ideas more concrete in terms of your own behavior. I am hopeful that you decided to take the time and exert the effort to try some of these exercises. The next chapter focuses on a different aspect of self-leadership, capitalizing on the "natural" rewards that come from performing attractive activities.

ENDNOTES

[1] An interesting book on this subject is by Carl E. Thoresen and Michael J. Mahoney, *Behavioral Self-Control* (New York: Holt, Rinehart and Winston, 1974).

[2] See, for example, Michael J. Mahoney and Diane B. Arnkoff, "Self Management: Theory, Research, and Application" in J. P. Brady and D. Pomerleau (eds.), *Behavioral Medicine: Theory and Practice* (New York: John Wiley, 1979); and Charles C. Manz and Henry P. Sims, Jr., "Self-Management as a Substitute for Leadership: A Social Learning Theory Perspective," *Academy of Management Review*, 5 (1980), 361–367. See also Chapter 2 in Charles C. Manz and Henry P. Sims, Jr., *SuperLeadership: Leading Others to Lead Themselves* (Englewood Cliffs, N.J.: Prentice Hall, 1989); (New York: Berkley [paperback], 1990).

[3] Alan Lakein, *How to Get Control of Your Time and Your Life* (New York: Signet, 1973).

4

Scenic Views, Sunshine, and the Joys of Traveling

or

Creating

the Self-Motivating Situation

One morning a national leader gazed in the mirror and knew his time had passed. He decided that he should select his successor. He believed this to be his most important remaining decision. Under his guidance, his tribe had grown from a small disorganized, self-defeating people into a powerful nation with much pride and sense of purpose.

So it was that he summoned his two greatest governors to his quarters—one of which he would choose as his successor. He turned to the first governor, whose accomplishments were great though significantly less than those of the other, and said, "Tell me of your philosophy of leadership and of how you have accomplished what you have."

The first governor responded quickly and simply, "I have learned the skill of getting my people to do what they should do whether they like it or not."

Then the national leader put the question to the second governor, whose physical stature and manner were considerably less impressive but who for some reason had accomplished significantly more.

The second governor had to think for a few moments and then answered in a manner that was not so clear and simple. "I'm not really a leader at all," he began.

The great national leader was concerned with this response and was beginning to think that the first governor was a more likely choice.

"There are your leaders," the second governor continued as he motioned to the crowds of citizens outside the building.

Now the great leader was more thoughtful and curious about the second governor's response though still unsure of its merit. All was quiet for some time and the great leader motioned to the crowd and asked, "Then what is the secret of their leadership?"

The second governor again responded slowly and thoughtfully. "They believe in what they are doing and for the most part enjoy doing it. You see, the secret to leading oneself is doing what one believes is worthwhile and doing so specifically because you believe in it and enjoy doing it. I'm just a coordinator of sorts. I simply try to help them discover what it is that they see as worthwhile and the capability, interest, and desire within them to do it. I find if I can help them get themselves pointed in the same purposeful, exciting direction, there is an unleashing of a tremendous power for progress.

Now the great leader thought awhile concerning the second governor's response with a sense of awe and wonder. "I have made my decision," he stated after a few moments.

All those inside and outside the chamber within hearing distance grew very silent straining to listen.

"For the future leadership of our nation, I have chosen these people!" he proclaimed while motioning with both hands to the crowds outside. And then turning to the second governor he said, "And you shall coordinate them."

This chapter is concerned with a naturally positive approach to self-leadership. The approach reminds me of a statement that a childhood doctor of mine used to frequently make: In response to a statement such as "Doctor, it hurts when I do this," he would say, "Then don't do that." This chapter is concerned with a principle involving similar logic, but that has a reversed focus. That is, if you say, "I like to do that," the parallel self-leadership response would be, "Then do it." Please don't misinterpret this discussion as a "do your own thing no matter what" message. Indeed, there are restrictions to this approach such as laws, your own values, and so on, that must be addressed. The primary purpose of this chapter, however, is to get across one simple idea: the desirability of using the natural rewards (your naturally motivating activities and tasks) toward the pursuit of more effective self-leadership. Hopefully, reading this book is shaping up to be this type of naturally rewarding activity as opposed to a "getting yourself to do a dreaded unattractive but necessary" type of task.

Take a few moments to assess your own tendencies regarding the use of natural rewards. Select the number in the following questionnaire that best describes your position in response to statements 1 through 15. As in the questionnaire in the previous chapter, some of the statements may seem quite similar—but respond to each one. Follow the directions provided for scoring your responses.

Self-Leadership Questionnaire 2 (SLQ2)
Self-Assessment Questionnaire for Creating
the Self-Motivating Situation

		Describes Me Very Well	Describes Me Well	Describes Me Somewhat	Does Not Describe Me Very Well	Does Not Describe Me At All
1.	I try to be aware of what activities in my work I especially enjoy	5	4	3	2	1
2.	When I have a choice, I try to do my work in places (a comfortable room, outdoors, etc.) that I like	5	4	3	2	1
3.	I seek out activities in my work that I enjoy doing	5	4	3	2	1
4.	I spend more time thinking about the good things rather than the drawbacks of my job	5	4	3	2	1
5.	I pay more attention to enjoyment of my work itself rather than rewards I will receive for doing it	5	4	3	2	1
6.	I know the parts of my job that I really like doing	5	4	3	2	1
7.	I try to arrange to do my work in pleasant surroundings when possible	5	4	3	2	1

Table (cont.)

		Describes Me Very Well	Describes Me Well	Describes Me Somewhat	Does Not Describe Me Very Well	Does Not Describe Me At All
8.	When I have a choice I try to do my work in ways that I enjoy rather than just trying to get it over with	5	4	3	2	1
9.	While I work I think less about things I don't like about my job than things I like	5	4	3	2	1
10.	My thinking focuses more on the things I like about actually doing my work than on benefits I expect to receive	5	4	3	2	1
11.	I can name the things I do in my job that I really enjoy	5	4	3	2	1
12.	When I can, I do my work in surroundings that I like	5	4	3	2	1
13.	I try to build activities into my work that I like doing	5	4	3	2	1
14.	I focus my thinking on the pleasant rather than the unpleasant feelings I have about my job	5	4	3	2	1
15.	I think less about the rewards I expect to receive for doing my job than on the enjoyment of actually doing it	5	4	3	2	1

Directions for scoring. Add the numbers you circled for each statement as indicated below to determine your score for each Self-Leadership Strategy.

Scores

A. Distinguishing natural rewards (add your responses for 1, 6, and 11) _____

B. Choosing pleasant surroundings (add your responses for 2, 7, and 12) _____

C. Building naturally rewarding activities into your work (add your responses for 3, 8, and 13) _____

D. Focusing on the pleasant aspects in your work (add your responses for 4, 9, and 14) _____

E. Focusing on natural rewards rather than external rewards (add your responses for 5, 10, and 15) _____

X. Total score (add the scores for A through E) _____

Interpreting your score. Your score for A through E suggests your current self-leadership tendencies concerning several self-leadership strategies that will be addressed in this chapter. Your score for each of these strategies could range from 3 (a total absence of the strategy in your current self-leadership) to 15 (a very high level of the strategy in your current self-leadership). Your score on A through E can be interpreted as follows:

1. A score of 3 or 4 indicates a *very low* level of the strategy
2. A score of 5 to 7 indicates a *low* level of the strategy
3. A score of 8 to 10 indicates a *moderate* level of the strategy
4. A score of 11 to 13 indicates a *high* level of the strategy
5. A score of 14 or 15 indicates a *very high* level of the strategy

Each of these strategies addressed by the questionnaire should generally contribute to personal performance and effectiveness. Therefore, a high score on A through E suggests a high level of self-leadership which offers potential to enhance performance. Each of the specific strategies is discussed in more detail throughout the remainder of the chapter.

Your score on X indicates your overall use of the self-leadership strategies and could range from a low of 15 to a high of 75. Your score on X can be interpreted as follows:

1. A score of 15 to 22 indicates a *very low* overall level of the strategies

2. A score of 23 to 37 indicates a *low* overall level of the strategies

3. A score of 38 to 52 indicates a *moderate* overall level of the strategies

4. A score of 53 to 67 indicates a *high* overall level of the strategies

5. A score of 68 to 75 indicates a *very high* overall level of the strategies

In general, a high score on X suggests that you possess some positive self-leadership tendencies. Your score on the questionnaire reflects what you believe your current self-leadership tendencies are. Regardless of your score, the remainder of this chapter is designed to help you implement and improve upon several self-leadership strategies. This chapter will provide you with a basis for better understanding and more effectively using the power of natural rewards.

THE NATURAL REWARDS

An important distinction has been emphasized in the psychology literature between two basic types of rewards.[1] One type of reward is the externally administered reward we most often identify regarding work organizations. A list of examples of this type of reward would include praise, a pay raise, time off, a promotion, an award of some kind, a bonus, and so on. In the previous chapter it was argued that many such rewards can be self-applied in order to influence positively our own motivation.

A second type of reward can also be identified that is generally less recognized and less understood, but that is no less important. This second type concerns rewards that are so closely tied to a given task or activity that the two cannot be separated. For example, an individual who enjoys reading the newspaper and spends a great deal of time doing so is engaging in an activity that could be described as naturally rewarding. No special externally administered or self-administered incentives are necessary to motivate this behavior. The incentives are built into the task itself. Of course, some externally applied rewards may result, such as compliments from others on being well informed. This emphasizes the fact that both types of rewards can be and often are at work at the same time. Still, the importance and power of these natural rewards should be recognized and, where possible, positively used.

In Chapter 2 it was suggested that an Olympic athlete could use many strategies to help motivate the difficult training behavior that accompanies success. It was also suggested that some of the necessary training may be naturally enjoyable—such as the natural enjoyment of pole vaulting for a decathlon athlete. This chapter is intended to suggest ways of harnessing the power of these naturally rewarding activities. It is designed to help us do what we want to do (and to like it) on our journey toward becoming what we choose for our lives.

WHAT MAKES ACTIVITIES NATURALLY REWARDING?

Two primary features can be identified as being descriptive of naturally rewarding activities: (1) They tend to make us feel more *competent* and (2) they tend to help us feel *self-controlling* (or self-determining).[2] In addition, another aspect of naturally rewarding activities will be suggested which concerns the sense of *purpose* we derive from them. The following discussion will address each of these features separately.

Feelings of Competence

One common aspect of naturally rewarding activities is that they frequently make us feel more competent. We often enjoy tasks that we perform well. People who perform well in a sport often like that sport; persons who do well in school often like school.

If we think of activities we especially like, we will probably find that many or most of them contribute to our feelings of competence in some way. For example, persons often enjoy talking about their work, hobbies, or some other area in which they possess knowledge and skill. If we find that a conversation we're having with another person is lagging, we might begin asking about her work or hobbies—a probable result is an increase of interest and enjoyment of the discussion for her. It can be argued that talking about a person's area of expertise contributes to her feelings of competence, and is therefore naturally rewarding. Perhaps you have noticed increased interest on your own part when you have talked to others about your skill areas. Similarly, as we improve our performance in an activity, we often find it becomes more enjoyable. A couple of good shots on the golf course, for example, can go a long way toward enticing us to play again in the future.

Of course, activities that tend to make us feel more competent are often tied to external rewards of some kind. Compliments from others on our display of knowledge in a conversation, and "oohs" and "aahs" for spectacular shots on the golf course will motivate us to continue these activities. The focus here, however, is on the naturally rewarding aspects of the activity itself. The feeling of strength and power for a runner who is in good condition can contribute to feelings of competence and be rewarding in itself, apart from trophies won and praise received for his/her efforts. The same logic applies to our activities in general.

Feelings of Self-Control

A second common characteristic of naturally enjoyable activities is that they frequently make us feel more self-controlling. There seems to be a natural human tendency in us to want to control our own destinies. From the toddler whose favorite activities seem to be the off-limits "no no's" to the adult who dreams of being his/her own boss and independently wealthy, the desire for personal control as opposed to external control is readily apparent.

We tend to desire to be a major force in determining what happens around us. For example, most of us would prefer to make important decisions that directly affect us, such as where we will live, where we will work, whom we will marry, and so forth, rather than to have someone else dictate these things to us. In a more general sense, we prefer to control aspects of our world rather than have them control us. Those of us who have been in situations where our every move seemed to be dictated by someone else, some rule or regulation, or some other external source know the helpless feelings of a lack of self-control. On the other hand, projects, hobbies, or other activities that we choose to undertake and in which we choose the method by which they will be performed contribute to our feelings of self-determination.

The combination of our desire for feelings of competence and self-control often results in a pattern in our behavior. This pattern involves a search for challenges that we are capable of overcoming, and then expended effort to overcome them. Increasing our running distance by an extra half mile, cutting a stroke off our golf game, or striving to achieve a reasonable increase in our performance rating at work all potentially reflect this kind of pattern. Grappling with reasonable challenges can be naturally rewarding because overcoming them can contribute to our feelings of competence and self-control. Activities that accomplish this result are probably prime candidates to try to increase or build into our tasks to make them more enjoyable. In essence I am suggesting that we use the potential effects of different activities on our feelings of competence and self-control as a guide for helping us select the features to build into our tasks, or to focus our thoughts on while performing them, to make our effort more naturally rewarding. These features will often take the form of a personal challenge of some sort that we are capable of overcoming.

Feelings of Purpose

One more important feature of naturally rewarding activities needs to be considered. This feature involves providing us with a sense of purpose. Even if a task makes us feel more competent and more self-controlling, we still may have a difficult time naturally enjoying and being motivated by it if we do not believe in its worthiness. As human beings we yearn for purpose and meaning. The troubling emergence of what has been frequently referred to as a "mid-life crisis" in many persons accents this idea. When looking back on one's life and looking ahead to the future, there is a basic need to feel what we are doing is of value. The best vacuum cleaner salesman in the world (who is obviously competent at what he does and who has freely chosen the profession, and is otherwise self-determining) may still not enjoy his work if he does not believe in what he is doing. But from where do feelings of purpose and meaning emerge?

One aspect of naturally rewarding activities that many would argue provides a sense of purpose, involves helping or expressing goodwill toward others. The term *altruism* is often used in connection with this idea. The author Hans Seyle has suggested the way to enjoy a rewarding lifestyle, free of disabling stress, is to practice "altruistic egoism."[3] In essence, this involves helping others and "earning their love" while at the same time recognizing one's own needs and enhancing oneself (egoism). Seyle explains that the natural biological nature of humankind drives people toward self-preservation, or what might be more bluntly described as *selfishness*. The philosophy suggests that only by marrying this innate, self-centered nature with an attitude of winning the goodwill and respect of others through altruistic efforts will a happy, meaningful life result. On the other hand, in a scholarly article analyzing evidence from biology and psychology, another author, Martin Hoffman, concludes that an altruistic motive may exist in humans apart from egoistic motives.[4] The evidence suggests that altruism may be a part of human nature that is not entwined with any "selfish" motive.

Regardless of why altruism can potentially add purpose to a task or, more generally, to one's life, it should not be overlooked. It may be the key to achieving feelings of purpose and meaning. We may never fully understand the altruistic urge, let alone human nature, but the essence of purpose may be centered in the simple idea of helping our fellow humans (and possibly *ourselves* in the process).

Of course, we can identify many pursuits that provide people with a feeling of purpose that at least appear to exist apart from altruistic motives. A scientist whose life purpose is encompassed in advancement of pure scientific knowledge exemplifies this idea. But then doesn't advancement of science potentially serve an altruistic end—the betterment of all people? Whether the scientist is significantly motivated by this aspect of his or her work may vary from person to person. The challenge is for each of us to search ourselves to find what provides us with a feeling of purpose. Altruism may well be at the heart of this search for most of us.

> The true destiny of man is to find his true destiny, and only then to obtain peace.

A checklist for guiding attempts to discover the natural rewards in your life follows. An exercise is provided to help you get started in identifying what your natural rewards are.

Checklist for Discovering Your Natural Rewards

☐ Discover your natural rewards

   ☐ Identify your tasks or activities that you naturally enjoy—
in which the rewards for doing them are built into, rather than
are separate from, the tasks themselves

   ☐ To help you find these naturally rewarding tasks, look for your
activities that:

      • Help make you feel competent

      • Help make you feel self-controlling

      • Provide you with a sense of purpose

   ☐

   ☐

Discovering Your Natural Rewards Exercise

Discover your naturally rewarding tasks (make notes).

1. List some of the activities that you naturally enjoy doing—
where the incentive for doing these activities is built into the tasks
rather than being separate from the tasks.

2. Classify the above activities and expand your list by identifying
activities that provide you with a sense of:
   a. Competence

   b. Self-control

   c. Purpose

3. Identify activities that accomplish all three (provide you with
a sense of competence, self-control, and purpose). Note
that activities that do not accomplish all three may not be
truly naturally rewarding activities.

TAPPING THE POWER OF NATURAL REWARDS

Two primary approaches to using natural rewards in order to enhance our self-leadership will be discussed here. These are (1) building more naturally enjoyable features into our life's activities, and (2) intentionally focusing our thoughts on the naturally rewarding aspects of our activities.

Building Natural Rewards Into Our Life's Activities

The blizzard hit the forest with a tremendous force, leaving a deep layer of new-fallen snow. The beaver was in a bad mood as he struggled toward the river. The snow made it hard to move and he was very irritable as he trudged along. Then the beaver noticed the whistling of the otter who was playfully sliding and rolling over slopes on his way to the river. "Why are you whistling on this horrible day?" snapped the beaver, obviously irritated. "Why, it's a great day," the otter sang out, "The best day I've had since yesterday—which was great, too." The beaver sneered at this response and continued to complain as he trudged forward. The otter continued to playfully slide and roll along, whistling while he went. They both reached the river.

The logic of the first approach to using natural rewards in exercising self-leadership involves identifying aspects of our endeavors that we naturally enjoy, and trying to increase these as much as is reasonably possible. For example, a business meeting can be held in an appealing location. The same matters addressed in a formal conference room of an office building will take on quite a different flavor when they are addressed in a relaxed meeting room at a beautiful resort. Similarly, a person who enjoys direct conversations with fellow employees can enjoy communicating a message face to face if he or she chooses rather than struggling to write a formal memo. The point is that we can usually identify several ways to accomplish many of our activities. By choosing to accomplish these tasks in more enjoyable ways, we are building in natural rewards for our efforts.

Let me illustrate these ideas further with the example of a person who runs or jogs regularly. This individual may run to obtain benefits such as increased endurance and strength, weight control, reduced stress, or the like. The individual may, on the other hand, run for the sheer enjoyment of the activity. I have a brother who has been a runner for many years—he takes his running seriously enough to play at it. Though he has trained hard and performed well in organized races, including marathons, he does not understand persons who run as a chosen form of leisure or exercise in a dull and monotonous way. A person who runs around a track day after day, probably through some force of will to get in shape, exemplifies this dull approach.

Natural rewards can be built into the activity to make it more enjoyable and more naturally rewarding if a runner chooses. One way to do this is to run in enjoyable places. Running along an ocean shore while listening to the peaceful rhythm of powerful white-crested waves and watching graceful sea gulls overhead can be an exhilarating experience. Or a person could run on a forest trail while listening to the singing of birds and the rushing of streams, and perhaps see an occasional squirrel, deer, or other wildlife. The running could be done in the early morning or at dusk while enjoying a brightly colored horizon. Running can be a more enjoyable experience for those runners who choose to make it so.

The emphasis to this point has been on the more obvious aspects of making activities more naturally enjoyable, that is, by choosing a pleasant context for the task which is, in essence, part of the task. Another focus involves following the guidelines suggested earlier: We can search for features of our activities that provide us with a feeling of competence, self-control, and purpose that are prime candidates for making a task more naturally rewarding. For a runner this might involve undertaking a reasonable challenge, such as a slightly longer run than usual over a challenging terrain. The task is all the better if it provides the runner with a sense of purpose because of a belief that he or she is setting a positive example and being an inspiration for others or the run is part of a fund-raising drive for charity, for example.

Similarly, our work and lives can be more naturally rewarding if we take them seriously enough to play at them and make them more enjoyable. One of my first experiences in my academic career was a conference I attended shortly after I began my doctoral studies. I was excited about the opportunity to listen to some of the most esteemed and respected faculty from across the country. At one of the first meetings of this gathering, doctoral students from dozens of universities (myself included) listened to perhaps the foremost scholar at the meeting present a rather bleak message: That we (the listening students) would never again have as light a workload as we had at that time. We were told by the speaker—and his comments were later supported by other speakers—that we should be prepared for very long and demanding work hours (perhaps 50, 60, 70, 80, or more hours a week) in our future careers. The listening students, many of whom already felt overworked, were obviously less than enthusiastic about this crystal ball view of their futures. While some of the rewarding aspects of our profession were discussed, the underlying message seemed to be, "If we really want to be successful, we should be prepared to work our tails off."

I have thought back to that experience many times. I was impressed with the speakers and feel that they were very competent people. For this reason I am all the more disturbed by the message conveyed and the effect it seemed to have on the audience. My problem with the philosophy presented (one that I believe is all too common) was that it seemed to suggest that the path to successful careers and the ultimate achievement of our life's goals is an agonizing, uphill climb. I do agree that sacrifices and intense effort are often integral parts of achieving one's goals (hence, the considerable value of self-discipline–oriented self-leadership strategies such as those presented in the last chapter). My underlying philosophy concerning achievement and success, however, is very different.

In essence I would argue that the road to success, while often rocky and challenging, should be made as naturally rewarding as possible. To the extent that a person pursues worthwhile challenges that are naturally enjoyed, a built-in motivation is established. We can explore our present work and life for the activities we enjoy that help us make progress toward our goals. We can build enjoyment into our work. We can plan our careers so that we enjoyably progress toward our desired destinies.

While I do believe that the speakers at the meeting I attended would agree with much of this logic, the message they conveyed, intentionally or unintentionally, conveyed a less pleasant view of work. Here's the message that has been developing and struggling for freedom from my mind since that meeting. "Fellow students of that meeting, don't work your tails off. Instead, work as little as possible, for when you are doing what you naturally enjoy, work is no longer work. Expend the effort and do put in the necessary hours, but build in natural rewards and work on what you believe in, in the way you most enjoy. Wherever possible do worthwhile things that you naturally like. Self-leadership strategies (such as those presented in the last chapter) can help us to overcome our formidable obstacles when they arise, but when there is a choice we should use the power of natural rewards. We can truly reach the pinnacle of success (and create a better world in the process) if our work is inspired. Let's choose a better tomorrow by choosing a better today." Amen.

Checklist for Building Natural Rewards into Your Activities

☐ Build natural rewards into your tasks

    ☐ Examine the nature of your current activities

    ☐ Identify pleasant contexts (places) in which you could perform your work that would make it more pleasant and naturally rewarding

    ☐ Identify activities that could be built into your tasks (e.g., different ways of accomplishing the same things) that make your work naturally rewarding (e.g., that provide you with a sense of competence, self-control, and purpose)

    ☐ Redesign your tasks by working in the contexts and building in the activities that make them more naturally enjoyable

    ☐

Building Natural Rewards into Your Activities Exercise

Follow these steps (make notes).

1. List some tasks that you need to do that you do not particularly enjoy doing.

2. Try to identify different, more pleasant contexts in which you could perform these tasks.

3. Identify activities that you find naturally rewarding that could possibly be built into the tasks (e.g., that provide you with a sense of competence, self-control, and purpose). Refer to the list that you developed in the "discovering your natural rewards exercise" as a starting point, and identify additional activities.

4. Redesign your tasks. Use your ideas from step 2 and step 3 as a basis for redesigning some of your tasks. Specify plans for redesigning tasks below, including contexts and activities that could make your work more naturally rewarding.

Focusing on the Natural Rewards

The three men were called crafters and worked side by side using the same tools and crafting the same items. The first man thought the sun was too hot, his tools were too old, and that his arms got too tired. He frowned and grumbled as he worked. The second man thought of the money he would receive on payday, the praise that would be bestowed upon him for his good work, and of being promoted to chief crafter one day. He did not think about his work much at all—only of his better future ahead. The third man thought of the pure, clean air that fed his lungs, of the feeling of power and strength he enjoyed as he worked his tools, and of the admiration he felt for the finely shaped item he was creating with his own hands. He smiled, for he was not working at all.

A second approach to tapping the power of natural rewards centers on the focus of our thoughts while we perform tasks. We can choose to think about, talk about, and, in general, focus on the parts of our work that we don't like—and thereby feel badly about our work. We can also choose to direct our focus on the rewards we expect to receive from performing our labor (money, praise, recognition) and thus be motivated by our images of the future. On the other hand, we can choose to direct our focus on the naturally enjoyable aspects of our work and enjoy the activity for its immediate value. It will be argued here that this latter focus is the key to naturally enjoying our present endeavors.

Most of our activities possess what we would consider both pleasant and unpleasant characteristics. A runner, for example, can think about heat and sweat, sore muscles and exhaustion, blisters, as well as a score of other things most would consider unpleasant. On the other hand, a runner can think about praise from others for his or her excellent physical condition, of a potentially longer life due to improved health, and the feeling of power and strength that accompanies a conditioned runner's stride. Both of these types of thoughts are available to a runner. Which type is chosen to focus on will significantly affect the runner's enjoyment of the activity.

This simple logic can be applied to our major activities in life. If we think for a moment about the various aspects of our work, we can probably identify several pleasant and unpleasant features. To bring these ideas to life, try the exercise provided on the next page.

**Focusing on Pleasant vs. Unpleasant Features
of Our Tasks Exercise**

Follow the steps provided below. Note that the logic of this exercise is very simple—the power of which can only be experienced by actually trying it. It is important that you take the time and exert the effort to try it out.

1. Identify and list several aspects of your work under the categories of Pleasant or Unpleasant provided below.

ASPECTS OF MY WORK

Pleasant   Unpleasant

2. Later, when you're at work, focus your thoughts for a while on the pleasant features you have identified. You might even try focusing your conversations with others on these features. Then switch your focus to the unpleasant features while you work.

3. Comment on the results of this exercise. How did you feel while you focused your thoughts on the pleasant aspects of your work? The unpleasant features? How did your focus affect your motivation and satisfaction with your work?

This exercise, though perhaps sounding overly simplistic emphasizes a crucial aspect of the importance of choice in self-leadership. Perhaps the most critical aspect of self-leadership concerns the way we choose to think about our tasks. The importance of our thinking patterns is considered in more detail in the remainder of this chapter and in Chapter 5. Suffice it to say here that if we believe that we do have freedom to choose what we wish to think about (if we do not possess freedom in our thoughts, it would seem that we possess no freedom at all), then choosing to focus on the pleasant aspects of our work, rather than the unpleasant, appears to be a logical strategy for helping us experience natural enjoyment.

There is still another issue that should be addressed. This issue centers on the question, "Does it make any difference what kind of pleasant features of our activities we focus our thoughts upon?" The position taken here is that it does. It was pointed out earlier that we can distinguish between rewards that are separable from a task and natural rewards that are built into a task and that largely derive from effects on our feelings of competence, self-determination, and purpose. By focusing on the former type of reward, our incentive for doing the task comes from the expectation of rewards at some future time. By focusing on the latter, our reason for doing the task is the task itself. This latter focus is the key to natural enjoyment of our work. These ideas suggest another simple exercise that is provided below.

If you are not able to identify naturally rewarding activities such as those suggested in the exercise, you are probably either in the wrong job or you're not sincerely trying to identify them. Focusing on rewards that are separate from the work should lead to motivation based on future expected benefits. Focusing on re-

---

Focusing on Different Types of Rewards Exercise

1.   List the rewarding aspects of your work under the following two categories. In the first category ("Separate from the work") list things like monetary incentives (such as salary and bonuses), praise and recognition received from superiors and fellow workers, possible promotion, awards, and so on. In the second category ("Part of the work") list things that are part of actually performing the work such as feelings of skill you experience while working, enjoyable interactions with people that help you accomplish tasks, fascinating learning that accompanies your performances, overcoming challenges, and so on.

<u>REWARDING ASPECTS OF MY WORK</u>

<u>Separate from the work</u>   <u>Part of the work</u>

2.   While at work focus your thoughts on the rewards listed under the category "Separate from the work" for a while, and then focus on rewards that are listed under the category "Part of the work."

3.   Comment on the results of this exercise. How did you feel while you focused on rewards that are separate from the work? Part of the work? How did your focus affect your motivation concerning your present efforts? Your future efforts? Your enjoyment of the task itself?

wards that are part of the work should result in an enhanced enjoyment of your present activities for their own sake.

What is being suggested, then, is not only to focus our thoughts on the rewarding aspects of our work, but further, to be selective in the kinds of rewards we focus on. Research evidence has been gathered indicating that when external rewards are increased for work that workers like, the workers may subsequently be motivated by the rewards rather than natural enjoyment of the task.[5] It may be that people reevaluate their reasons for doing enjoyable work when external rewards are emphasized. Receiving the rewards may consequently take precedence over natural enjoyment of the activities. While this viewpoint has been controversial among researchers, a fairly substantial body of evidence has been accumulated to support it. The significance of this viewpoint for the present discussion is that focusing our thoughts on expected external rewards may undermine our immediate enjoyment of the task. While such a focus may be useful for some tasks that do not possess many naturally enjoyable qualities, focusing on natural rewards is preferable to optimize the enjoyment of our present activities.

A checklist to help guide efforts toward achieving motivation through focusing on the natural rewards is provided below. Take a moment to look over this checklist and to reflect on how you can take advantage of the power of natural rewards in your future activities.

Checklist for Focusing on the Natural Rewards

☐ Focus your thoughts on the natural rewards

    ☐ Identify the pleasant, enjoyable aspects of your tasks

    ☐ Distinguish between the rewarding aspects of your work that are separable from the work itself, and those rewarding aspects that are part of (built into) your work

    ☐ Focus your thoughts on the pleasant rather than the unpleasant aspects of your tasks while you work

    ☐ Where possible, focus your thoughts on the rewards that are part of (not separate from) the actual task to obtain motivation and satisfaction for your immediate efforts

☐ Work toward developing the ability and habit of distinguishing and focusing on the natural rewards in your work

(*Note*: The intention of this strategy is not to ignore our problems and concerns. Important negative issues regarding our work need to be dealt with. On the other hand, while we actually exert effort, focusing our thoughts on the naturally rewarding aspects of our tasks can provide motivational and emotional benefits, including those occasions when we must deal with problems and concerns that are part of the job.)

☐

☐

A CLOSING COMMENT

Before leaving this chapter, a comment should be made concerning the relationship, and perhaps the seeming contradictions between the ideas of the present chapter and Chapter 3. The present chapter has emphasized natural rewards built into a task, while Chapter 3 suggested several self-applied techniques, including the use of self-applied rewards that are separable from the task. Both approaches were presented as ways to achieve more effective self-leadership. Actually, the strategies of the two chapters can complement each other very well. Strategies such as those presented in Chapter 3 can be used in especially difficult situations that are lacking in natural rewards. The intention is to maintain the self-leadership necessary to work through the difficult and unattractive but necessary tasks on the way to activities and future job positions that we can naturally enjoy. In the meantime, an effort should be made to build in and focus on the natural rewards that are available. To the extent that this can be accomplished, greater enjoyment of our present moments can be obtained.

Consider the following case. It was developed from some of the experiences of participants in my training programs and courses (e.g., managers, executives, and MBA students) who actually applied the kinds of strategies presented in this chapter.

The Case of The External Rewards That Were Just Not Enough

Anne was a staff manager in a large American corporation. She had a generally strong track record and was known to be a hard worker who completed her assignments on time. She was not considered to be especially creative or innovative, but she was dependable. In performing her job, Anne relied heavily on the directions and cues she received from her boss, the department manager, Bob Jones. The past performance reviews Anne received from Bob were strong but not outstanding.

This was the occasion of Anne's third performance review since she had joined the department. As Anne looked over the review form Bob had just handed her, she couldn't help thinking that it looked familiar. This feeling was soon confirmed. "As you probably realize, Anne, your performance rating this year is essentially the same as last year," Bob stated. "Once again you have turned in a strong performance and you are showing steady progress in your department. I think any recommendation for promotion is still a ways off but keep up your hard work and dependability and you'll get there eventually."

Anne felt pretty satisfied with the way the review had gone and with the overall evaluation she had received. But when Bob asked "Is there anything else you'd like to talk about?" she decided to raise an issue that was troubling her.

"Bob, there is one thing that is bothering me."

"What's that, Anne?"

"Well, I seem to be losing interest in my job. I'm not sure that I'm very motivated by it any more. At first I was really challenged by it and was anxious to perform my best. Now I'm not so sure I like what I'm doing. I'm just not sure I'm having much fun anymore."

A surprised look came over Bob's face. He hadn't really expected any response to his final question, and now he kind of regretted that he had asked it at all. "Do you have any suggestions or ideas on how to deal with the problem?" Bob asked in voice that sounded a little confused and unsure.

Anne paused for a moment but then decided to say what she was really thinking. "Well I've been doing some reading and I ran across an article that suggested that we should redesign our own jobs. The main idea is to change what we do and how we do it so that it better fits our strengths and interests while still meeting our responsibilities. I've been thinking about this for a few days now and I've decided I'd like to try it if it's OK with you. You see, at first it was enough to follow your directions and to receive your approval when I got a job done. Now I'd like to contribute more of my creativity and innovative abilities and tailor my job to fit me a little better."

Bob was a bit unsure of all that Anne was saying, but he could tell she felt strongly about these ideas. Since she had always been a dependable employee, he agreed to let her try this new strategy, although he wasn't quite sure what to expect.

Over the next few weeks, a significant change came over Anne. At first she was a bit cautious about making changes and initiating things more on her own, but gradually she started coming up with new ideas. She developed a new computerized tracking system for organizing the department's work projects (she liked working on computers). She also created a weekly report form that she used to keep Bob informed of her progress on the specific projects she was working on. This weekly report took the place of her usually multiple visits to Bob's office everyday to seek his guidance. She found that these kinds of accomplishments gave her a feeling of increased competence in her work. And checking in with Bob much less often gave her a sense of having more control over her own activities. Also, as Anne saw her new computer tracking system being used by other people in the department (and some even followed her example in using the weekly progress report form), she felt an increased sense of purpose because of the benefits she was providing for others.

Over time Anne became known as one of the most creative and enthusiastic employees in the division. When her next performance review rolled around, Anne looked with satisfaction at the review form Bob handed to her on which she was rated as an outstanding performer and recommended for a promotion. As she scanned the form, a puzzled look came over her face. "Did you make a mistake in identifying my job position?" she asked Bob.

"No, not really, Anne. In my book you are no longer a staff administrator. You are an advanced project manager. I made a special request for this job title change and a raise in grade for you. That's partly why you're getting this big raise," Bob said with a smile as he leaned over and showed her the sizable pay increase she was to receive recorded on a sheet of paper. You see, I've recommended you for a more significant promotion, but in the meantime you've already been promoted."

Anne beamed as she took all this good news in. But then she stopped and got a serious look on her face. "You know, Bob, thinking back over what has happened in the past year, the thing I value most is how I feel about my work. I was kind of confused when we met a year ago. I really wanted to like my job more for its own value. Now I really like what I do. Thanks for the pay raise and title change, but I've got to be honest." She paused and looked him right in the eye for emphasis. "I'd probably be excited about the coming year even if you had given me a minimal raise and didn't recommend that I be promoted. I've designed a job that really fits me, that I'm good at, that I enjoy, and through which I can really make contributions that benefit others. I can't wait to see what I can accomplish this year."

The inspirational writer Norman Vincent Peale, who has been read by and has affected the thinking and living of millions of people, made a statement in one of his books that parallels the major thrust of this chapter quite closely. He said, "Do your job naturally, because you like it, and success will take care of itself."[6] If we practice a self-leadership style that allows us natural enjoyment of our activities, we can indeed derive the motivation we need to be successful—especially at enjoying life.

ENDNOTES

[1] See Edward Deci, *Intrinsic Motivation*, (New York: Plenum, 1975).

[2] See, for example, ibid.; and Edward Deci and Richard Ryan, "The Empirical Exploration of Intrinsic Motivational Processes," in L. Berkowitz (ed.), *Advances in Experimental Social Psychology*, vol. 13, 1980.

[3] Hans Seyle, *Stress Without Distress*, (New York: Signet Books, 1974).

[4] Martin L. Hoffman, "Is Altruism Part of Human Nature?" *Journal of Personality and Social Psychology*, vol. 40 (1981), 121–137.

[5] See, for example, Deci, *Intrinsic Motivation*; and Edward Deci, John Nezlek, and Louise Sheinman, "Characteristics of the Rewarder and Intrinsic Motivation of the Rewardee," *Journal of Personality and Social Psychology*, 40 (1981), 1–10.

[6] Norman Vincent Peale, *A Guide to Confident Living*, (Greenwich, Conn.: Fawcett Crest Books, 1948), p. 59.

5

Travel Thinking
or
Redesigning
Our Psychological Worlds

The traveler physically collapsed and groaned with relief as he gazed upon the white-haired old man who sat before him. He paused for a moment to cautiously look over the sheer cliff he had just climbed to reach the top of the mountain. He gazed upon the thick jungle beyond that had been his home for many days. "Old man," he gasped, "I have traveled for days to speak to you because many have said you are among the wisest of all the living. "I must know the true nature of life—is it good or is it bad?"

The white-haired old man responded with a question of his own. "Tell me first—how do you see life, my son?"

The traveler looked away, frowning, and said slowly and sadly, "I believe life is bad—people are selfish and basically cruel, and fate always seems anxious to deliver a disheartening blow." Then he turned to the old man and asked, with obvious anguish in his voice, "Is this the nature of life?"

"Yes," responded the old man, "This is the nature of life, my son."

The traveler dropped his gaze, his face going blank, pulled himself to his feet, and solemnly began his descent back down the cliff.

A few moments later another traveler pulled himself up over the edge of the cliff and collapsed at the feet of the white-haired old man. "Tell me, old man of much wisdom," he gasped, "What is the nature of life? Is it good or is it bad?"

The old man again asked the question, "Tell me first—how do you see life, my son?"

At this question the traveler looked hopefully into the old man's eyes. "Life can be hard, and the way is often difficult," he started, "but I believe the nature of life is basically good. People are not perfect, but I see much value in the heart of each I meet—even those that would be called the most lowly. I believe life is challenge and growth, and offers a sweet victory for those that try and endure. "Is this the nature of life?" he asked as he continued his hopeful stare into the old man's eyes.

"Yes," responded the old man, "This is the nature of life, my son."

The emphasis of this chapter is on our unique psychological worlds. The viewpoint taken is that each of us experiences a uniquely different psychological world, even when faced with the same physical situations, because of the way we think. Our senses (sight, hearing, feeling, tasting, smelling, and perhaps other more mystical senses) are constantly bombarded with stimuli. If you check yourself right this minute, you are likely to find you have a potentially overwhelming number of things to focus on. What sights and what sounds are available to you, both near and distant? By the way, how do the bottom of your feet feel? Are they tired, sore, comfortable? What kinds of things have you thought about lately? Have you spent more mental energy thinking about your problems or your opportunities?

The point is that we usually have a choice regarding what we focus on and what we think about. We can't deal with every possible stimulus that we come in contact with, nor can we deal with every possible thought. Of course, we don't have much of a choice about some of our thoughts, such as those we experience when struck by unexpected physical pain, but we *do* have a choice regarding what we think about much of the time. In addition, the things we choose to think about can be thought of in different ways. That is what this chapter is all about: what we choose to think about and how we choose to think about it. This may sound a little silly, but it is probably the most important part of self-leadership. So let's spend a little more time thinking about how we think.

Take a moment to complete the short self-assessment exercise that follows. Choose the letter of the statement (a or b) that you agree with more for each pair presented (1 through 10).

1. a.   There is a real opportunity built into every problem.
   b.   Anything that can go wrong will.
2. a.   A bird in the hand is worth two in a tree.
   b.   Real opportunities are worth sticking your neck out for.
3. a.   Most people cannot be counted on.

    b.   Every person is a valuable resource in some way.

4. a.   Difficulties make us grow.

    b.   Difficulties beat us down.

5. a.   The world is full of impossibilities.

    b.   Nothing is impossible that we can conceive of.

6. a.   When half of the days in an enjoyable vacation have passed I still have half of my vacation to enjoy.

    b.   When half of the days in an enjoyable vacation have passed my vacation is half over.

7. a.   The best approach to dealing with energy shortages is conservation.

    b.   The best approach to dealing with energy shortages is to develop new energy sources.

8. a.   Life after death.

    b.   Death after life.

9. a.   Failure is an opportunity to learn.

    b.   Failure is a negative outcome to effort.

10. a.   Happiness is the absence of problems.

    b.   Problems are the spice of life.

Directions for scoring. Circle the choice you made (a or b) for each pair of statements (1 through 10) below. Total the number of letters circled in each column.

	I	II
1.	a	b
2.	b	a
3.	b	a
4.	a	b
5.	b	a
6.	a	b
7.	b	a
8.	a	b
9.	a	b
10.	b	a

TOTAL   _____   _____

              opportunity   **obstacle**
              thinking   **thinking**

Interpreting your score. The short exercise you have just completed was designed to help you assess your current pattern of thinking. It focuses on two distinct types of thinking patterns discussed later in this chapter: opportunity thinking and obstacle thinking. The scores that you recorded for column I and column II (the maximum possible total for either is, of course, 10) suggest your current thinking tendencies. That is, if your column I total was higher than column II, your score indicates that your current thinking patterns tend to reflect opportunity thinking more than obstacle thinking (the reverse would be true if your column II total was higher than column I). The greater the difference between the two totals, the more you tend toward one pattern or the other. In general, a higher score on column I than column II reflects some desirable self-leadership tendencies, while a higher score for column II may indicate some fundamental problems.

Of course, as was the case for the self-assessment questionnaires in Chapters 3 and 4, your results on this exercise should be interpreted cautiously. The way you score may reflect your current mood or outlook as opposed to any long-term tendencies. On the other hand, an exercise such as this is useful in helping you reflect on the pattern of thinking that you tend to adopt in thinking about and approaching situations.

The remainder of this chapter is devoted to providing a foundation for increasing your understanding of and improving your patterns of thinking (your psychological world). Several strategies will be suggested that provide a basis for developing more desirable patterns of thought through which you see and deal with the world.

OUR PSYCHOLOGICAL WORLDS

What we experience in life is unique. No one else in the world can experience exactly what we do. We create our own psychological worlds by selecting what enters our minds (where the essence of human experience takes place) and what shape it takes after it does. The content of our unique psychological worlds determines the way we behave, and our behavior helps determine the nature of our physical worlds. All of these things together determine our progress toward our personal destinies. These ideas are represented pictorially in Figure 5-1.

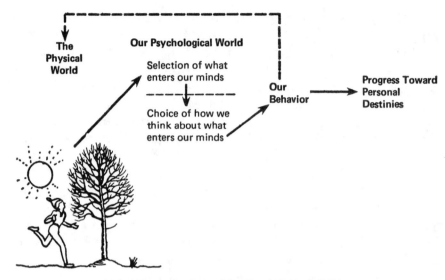

FIGURE 5-1. The Role of Our Psychological Worlds

We carry in our minds a world that is more real to us than the physical one within which we live. A cold winter blizzard has a different meaning to an avid skier than it does to an avid golfer. Identical physical conditions can result in joyful exultation for one person and depression and gloom for another. In fact, we are quite capable of turning potentially joyful, motivating situations into those of demoralizing gloom through our thoughts and resulting actions. For example, if we are invited to a social gathering of some kind, we can experience the event as an unhappy one by being overly self-conscious about our appearance and what we say. In essence we would be choosing to focus our mind on negative aspects of a potentially very positive situation. In general, we can look for the positive or negative in people and situations, and as a result create the psychological atmosphere in which we live and experience life.

Also, since our actions help to shape the physical world within which we live, our psychological worlds ultimately have an impact on the physical world itself. In fact, the way we think about the physical world can be self-fulfilling. If we attend a social gathering worrying that we will not be accepted or liked by those present, we can make this fear come true. By being withdrawn and closed to others, these others are likely to reciprocate with similar behavior.

The remainder of this chapter will address different ways of analyzing and dealing with the way we think and how this affects our own self-leadership. The intention is to increase our understanding of and ability to deal with our psychological worlds. We can change our psychological worlds and our resulting behavior and experiences if we choose to do so. This viewpoint is consistent with psychological perspectives that place the responsibility for our actions and self-improvement where it belongs: on ourselves.[1] If we wish to achieve effective self-leadership and obtain personal effectiveness, we need to take responsibility for what we think and do. This approach is in direct contrast to the common tendency to place the responsibility for our actions on external sources such as authority figures, or traumatic experiences from our childhoods. The focus is on dealing with and improving our immediate thinking and behavior rather than looking for reasons (excuses) for why we can't become what we wish to and are capable of becoming.

IS THERE POWER IN POSITIVE THINKING?

In the 1950s a view toward more effective living was written about and read by many persons. This viewpoint, which can be called *positive thinking*, was introduced by the Reverend Norman Vincent Peale. Several books were published, including the well-known bestseller, *The Power of Positive Thinking*.[2] Dr. Peale subsequently reported numerous cases in which persons overcame challenges and obstacles with the aid of positive thinking, in support of his ideas.[3] Peale's work, however, was never subjected to what authorities in the area of psychology and human behavior would describe as scientific research. In fact, until recently, most academics in these areas would likely have considered his work with some amusement. Nevertheless, the effects of his work gained widespread public notoriety and attention such as few authors ever receive. And, more recently, evidence has begun to accumulate in support of the many benefits to be gained from positive thinking.[4]

The idea of positive thinking is a useful reference point from which to consider improvement of our psychological worlds. Several different elements that offer potential to help explain how our thinking can have an impact on our behavior and experience of life will be considered. These include our beliefs, our imagined experiences, our self-instruction (self-talk), the personal "scripts" we act out in our daily living, and our thought patterns. The underlying logic is that if we make systematic efforts to change our thinking in beneficial ways, we can improve our self-leadership. Beneficial thinking (or positive thinking, if you prefer) offers the potential to help us to improve our personal effectiveness just as beneficial *behaving* does. In fact, as mentioned earlier, our behavior and our unique ways of thinking (mental behavior) are two primary, inter-related features in the total influence picture (see Figure 2-2).

Beliefs

In 1954, a physical feat that was thought to be humanly impossible was achieved. Roger Banister ran the mile in four minutes. Since then dozens of runners have accomplished this challenge that had eluded others for so long. Banister later ex-pressed the view that a new mental outlook for runners was responsible for these accomplishments, rather than improvements in running equipment or techniques. Once people believed it was possible to run a mile in less than four minutes, a major barrier to its accomplishment was removed.

The idea that what we can conceive of, or believe is possible, can be achieved is not new. The amazing fulfillment of many predictions made in books that have attempted to describe the future, such as *Future Shock, Brave New World*, and *1984*, suggests that what we believe can happen *can* happen.

In fact, one perspective for dealing with our personal behavior and emotional reactions in an attempt to improve them involves focusing on the beliefs we possess.[5] The argument is that it is our beliefs, rational or irrational, that determine our reactions to ex-ternal events and ultimately the quality of our life experiences. If we possess irrational fears or hang-ups, these negative personal characteristics can be traced to irrational beliefs. It is not the external event that causes our reaction to it, but instead our beliefs about that event. According to this view, only by recognizing, confronting, and altering these beliefs can we improve our behavior and mental outlook. Figure 5-2 displays this idea pictorially.

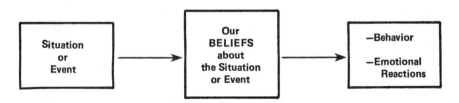

FIGURE 5-2. The Importance of Beliefs

For example, imagine for a moment that we have a strong fear of speaking in front of groups. Further, suppose that we would like to overcome this fear and become a competent and confident public speaker. One way of dealing with the apprehensions we possess is to try to discover and alter the beliefs that underlie this fear. Beliefs that might lead to such a fear could include a belief that people will think less of us if we do not express ourselves articulately, or a belief that others know more than we do so we would only display our ignorance by speaking. Once identified, effort could then be made to examine and discover the irrationality of these beliefs and ultimately to eliminate or replace them with more constructive beliefs. When among friends, for example, an informal, imperfect style of speaking is not likely to lead them to a devaluation of our friendship. Also, while others may know more about some subjects than we do, there are likely several subjects in which we would be the expert in the group. By examining the beliefs we hold that are hindering our self-leadership and dealing with them, as in the previous example, increased personal effectiveness may well result.

A checklist for guiding attempts at examining and improving your belief system follows. Also, a short exercise is provided to help you get started in making such improvements.

Checklist for Analyzing and Enhancing Your Belief System

- [ ] Improve your belief system
    - [ ] Identify the types of tasks and activities for which your beliefs are especially important (significantly impact on your actions and feelings)
    - [ ] Analyze the accuracy of your beliefs
    - [ ] Question whether your beliefs positively or negatively affect your actions and feelings
    - [ ] Isolate your inaccurate, dysfunctional beliefs and challenge them
    - [ ] Identify more positive functional beliefs to take their place
    - [ ]
    - [ ]

Enhancing Your Belief System Exercise

Analyze and enhance your belief system (make notes).

1. Identify some of the more challenging problems or tasks that you have been faced with recently (try to think of occasions where your beliefs/judgments were especially important)—especially those occasions where your results were unsatisfactory.

2. How did your beliefs affect your actions and reactions in these situations? (For example, did your beliefs positively/negatively affect your chosen course of action? How?)

3. Were your beliefs accurate? (Of course, hindsight always seems to be 20/20, but try to rationally search for patterns in your beliefs on these occasions that were dysfunctional as well as those that were constructive.)

4. Identify some more functional, constructive beliefs that you might have substituted for your dysfunctional ones on these occasions. How might your actions have changed if they were based on these alternative beliefs? How might your results have changed?

As another simple exercise analyze and manage your beliefs to help you through current difficult situations. When you find yourself reacting destructively to difficult situations (e.g., an argument with a coworker or spouse), try to list on paper the beliefs or assumptions that underlie your reactions. Next try to list alternative, more constructive, beliefs or assumptions for each one you have listed.

Imagined Experience

Mary was gliding cautiously across the shimmering ice when one of her skates struck a hard lump on the otherwise smooth surface. Her weight shifted quickly forward and she found herself flying through the air. She landed hard on her shoulder and right cheek, and felt pain go through her body. Her collarbone had been severely fractured and she noticed blood trickling from a cut on her cheek. Then she heard a loud crack and the ice began to separate underneath her. A moment later she could scarcely breathe because of the icy cold water that enveloped her body. The extreme pain in her shoulder made it impossible for her to swim. She gulped water in an attempt to breathe. A desperate sense of panic swept over her, and ...

"Mary are you going to put your skates on or do I have to do it for you," asked Bill impatiently.

Mary stood up nervously, and turning to walk away said, "I don't think I want to learn to skate today; maybe some other time."

The theme of this chapter centers around the idea that each of us experiences unique psychological worlds. These inner worlds at any given moment may or may not accurately represent external realities. We can create and, in essence, symbolically experience imagined results of our behavior before we actually perform. When faced with a specific situation, our past learning and beliefs we hold help shape what we expect to occur if we take different actions. Two different persons faced with the same situation, such as ice skating for the first time, can react differently because of their imagination of expected experiences.

For example, two new salespersons about to make their first sales call can mentally experience through their imaginations the event before it occurs. Suppose one salesperson experiences images of a muddled presentation which results in humiliating rejection from the client. This imagined experience could potentially block effective performance. In fact, such self-defeating images can promote corresponding negative results. The resulting lack of confidence and unconvincing presentation could lead to the very failure that was imagined. Suppose the second salesperson imagines a positive experience resulting in a sizable sale and a worthwhile experience for both parties. In this case the individual would likely possess a higher level of confidence going into the presentation and a higher probability of success.

The point is that we are capable of creating a unique world within ourselves. The essence of our experience of life is centered within the inner world we create. Many would agree that imagination of the pain and suffering we expect from a visit to the dentist is often, and perhaps usually much worse, than the actual event. The imagined negative experience may last for days prior to the actual appointment which is over within minutes. Also, our imagined positive experiences can be more striking and powerful than their occurrence in the physical world. Anticipated events are often disappointing when they finally take place because they do not live up to our expectations. A party may not be as enjoyable as we imagined it would be, nor a vacation we planned for months. Production of films based on classic novels often fall short of the original work. This is because of the richness we can add to the book with our imaginations that film makers can rarely achieve in visual form.

Symbolic, imagined experiences are an important component of the psychological worlds in which we interpret and experience life. If we can discover the effect they have on our lives, we can gain a better understanding of ourselves. We may find, for example, that before undertaking new challenges we usually imagine negative results. To deal with this habitual negative thinking we could intentionally imagine positive results before we take actions. Imagining a receptive, appreciative audience rather than a critical, hostile one before giving a speech, for example, may significantly help us to overcome a fear of public speaking. By exercising greater choice and control over our imagined experiences, we can improve the quality of our psychological worlds and, potentially, our personal effectiveness.

A checklist to help you make improvements in your imagined experiences follows along with a short exercise to help you get started making the changes that you see as desirable.

Checklist for Improving Your Imagined Experience Tendencies

☐ Use your imagination to facilitate desirable performance

   ☐ Analyze your current imagined experience tendencies. Ask yourself questions such as:

- Do they focus on positive or negative outcomes of challenging tasks?

- Do they generally facilitate or hinder my confidence and performance of tasks?

- Are they realistic? Reasonable?

☐ Identify destructive imagined experience tendencies such as the tendency to habitually and unrealistically imagine negative results for your actions

☐ Work to eliminate these destructive thought patterns by choosing to think about other things

☐ Purposefully choose to imagine sequences of events and outcomes that help clarify and motivate (rather than hinder) your efforts (for example, once you have chosen a course of action and are committed to it, motivate yourself by imagining positive rather than negative results of your efforts)

☐

Improving Your Imagined Experience Tendencies Exercise

Follow the steps below.

1. Think about some recent challenges you have faced that especially provoked your imagination regarding the different actions you could take and the likely consequences of these different actions. Also, check yourself throughout the next few days as you face new challenges such as these.

2. Explore the nature of your imagined experiences on these occasions. Are they realistic? Do they tend to focus on the positive or the negative? Are they constructive?

3. Analyze the specific instances you identified in step 1 regarding the effect your imagination is having on your performance. What effect is your imagination having on your decisions (such as your willingness to take risks)? How is your imagination affecting your confidence and motivation?

4. Purposefully use your imagined experience to enhance your performance when facing new challenges. When facing problems that provoke your imagination, choose to keep your images constructive; reasonably realistic and positive. This will take work, since it will likely mean changing ingrained, habitual ways of thinking—here the practice of self-leadership (e.g., using the strategies presented in Chapter 3) becomes important in working to achieve yet further improvements in your self-leadership abilities.

Self-Talk

The crowd of more than 500 people applauded politely the introduction of Betty Smith to speak. Betty thought to herself, "Oh, God, there are so many people here. I'm really nervous. I wish I could hide somewhere." As she reached the podium, she took a deep breath. "No, I have to be calm. I can do it. I'm well prepared for this talk and I am a good speaker—I'll do the best I can and try to enjoy it."

The crowd rose to its feet and applauded loudly at the end of the speech. Betty felt exhilarated. "I did it," she thought. "That was fun and I did a good job. Why have I been so afraid of speaking to groups? I'm good at it."

An important part of our psychological worlds that is related to beliefs and imagined experiences is self-talk. Although our immediate reaction to observing someone talking to themselves is that they are being a bit crazy, we all talk to ourselves. Usually our self-dialogues take place at a mental, unobservable level; that is, we self-instruct, evaluate, and react to ourselves mentally. For example, when conversing with others, if we say something we wish we hadn't, we are likely to think something like, "Oh, God—why did I say that? That was stupid." On the other hand, if we say something that we approve of, we might think, "I'm sounding pretty good—I'm really speaking well." The point is we *do* carry on internal dialogues, and probably at times talk to ourselves out loud.

One way to improve our self-leadership, and in turn our personal effectiveness, is to learn to speak to ourselves more effectively. A psychologist stated that therapists do change what clients say to them; now it's time that they make use of their influence "to change what clients say to themselves."[6] Improving self-talk has already been used as an approach to help persons overcome various forms of anxiety, to improve creativity, and to deal with other types of human problems. A number of procedures have been used to accomplish these results.[7]

One procedure we can use involves engaging in constructive self-talk aloud as we perform a challenging task. By learning to instruct, reassure, praise, and otherwise verbally direct our own behavior, we can improve our task performance as well as our feelings about what we do. Ultimately the constructive self-talk is internalized so that we learn to use it constructively and silently in our minds. Such a procedure has been used to help persons overcome personal problems, with the added feature of having a model person display constructive self-talk first.[8] That is, after watching someone else use effective self-talk, an observer tries similar behavior himself.

One particularly appropriate application of effective self-talk deals with the many types of stress that exist within our complex, fast-paced society. By learning to reassure and talk our way through stressful situations, we can improve our personal effectiveness. One approach to developing this ability involves practice. By practicing constructive self-talk in stressful situations, a person can gradually learn to improve her ability to deal with stress. If we were new salespersons who experience anxiety during sales presentations, we could, for example, practice constructive self-talk (not aloud, but mentally, of course) during several actual presentations. The steps that might be used could include (1) *prepare* (e.g.,ask ourselves what needs to be done, and focus on constructive mental preparation for the presentation; (2) *confront* (e.g., face the situation, focus on doing one step at a time, and reassure ourselves that we can handle the challenge); (3) *cope* (e.g., when the stress arises, remind ourselves that it is normal and only temporary, and instruct ourselves to relax and focus on the task at hand; (4) *self-reward* (praise ourselves for having faced the situation and having coped with it, recognizing any improvements we are making while reminding ourselves that improvement should help us achieve future success).

Each of these steps would be accomplished through the use of various self-statements that we find personally beneficial. For example, at the confronting stage, mental self-statements—"I can do it," "I can overcome this situation," "I know what needs to be done and I'm ready," "I will succeed"—could be used. This procedure can be adapted and used in almost any situation that we find stressful. Whether our focus is on sales calls, presentations to groups, confronting intimidating people, or going to the dentist, we can learn to cope better and improve our performance in the future by practicing and developing constructive internal dialogues while in these threatening situations.

The idea of learning to talk to ourselves may sound like a strange way to improve our self-leadership and our personal effectiveness. The important thing to remember, however, is that we all talk to ourselves, and probably in many instances in a self-defeating manner. By improving our self-talk we can take a major step toward improving the psychological worlds in which we live. We spend a great deal of time thinking about and worrying about what we say to others. It's time we focus on what we say to ourselves.

A checklist to help you make desirable changes in your self-talk patterns follows. An exercise is included to help you get started in making the changes you would like to make.

Developing Effective Self-Talk Exercise

Develop constructive self-talk (make notes).

1. Over the next few days pay attention to your self-talk. Make notes regarding your self-dialogue using a record sheet similar in design to the one suggested below.

Event	Nature of your self-talk (Constructive? Positive or negative?)	How did your self-talk influence your actions?

2. In what ways could you improve your self-talk tendencies? What kinds of self-statements have you discovered that you would like to eliminate? How could you improve the effectiveness of your self-dialogues? (For example, what kinds of self-statements do you believe could help you successfully overcome challenges such as those you identified in step 1?)

3. Practice constructive self-talk. Try talking yourself through some difficult challenges (try practicing aloud first—preferably in private, of course—and then silently in your thoughts). Make notes regarding your experiences.

Event	Nature of the self-statements you used	Results (what impact did your self-talk seem to have on your confidence, motivation, performance, etc.)?

4. Use self-talk to help you meet future important challenges. Use it to help you prepare for, confront, cope with, and reward yourself for meeting upcoming challenges. Keep a self-observation sheet handy to help you monitor and maintain constructive self-dialogues over time.

Event	Nature of Self-Statements	Impact on Your Results

Checklist for Using Self-Talk to Your Advantage

☐ Use self-talk to your advantage

    ☐ Analyze your current self-talk tendencies. Ask yourself:

        • Is my self-talk constructive?

        • Does it motivate and facilitate my performance?

    ☐ Identify negative types of self-talk that you would like to eliminate, and more constructive self-statements that you would like to develop

    ☐ Practice constructive self-talk—aloud at first, and then internalize it (i.e., use constructive, self-instructional, self-motivational internal speech)

    ☐ Purposefully use self-talk to your advantage when faced with challenges (talk yourself through your challenges). Use it to help you prepare for, confront, cope with, and reward yourself for dealing with your difficulties

    ☐

    ☐

Thought Patterns

A man is what he thinks about all day long.
RALPH WALDO EMERSON

The previous discussion addressed several factors that help shape our unique psychological worlds. One way of picturing these ideas is to view our internal psychological selves in terms of thought patterns. That is, we tend to develop certain ways of thinking about our experiences. We might say that just as we develop habitual ways of behaving, we develop habitual ways of thinking. These thought patterns involve, among other things, our beliefs, our imagined experiences, and our self-talk. Figure 5-3 presents these ideas pictorially. It shows how our beliefs, our imagined experiences, and our self-talk all influence one another and help to shape

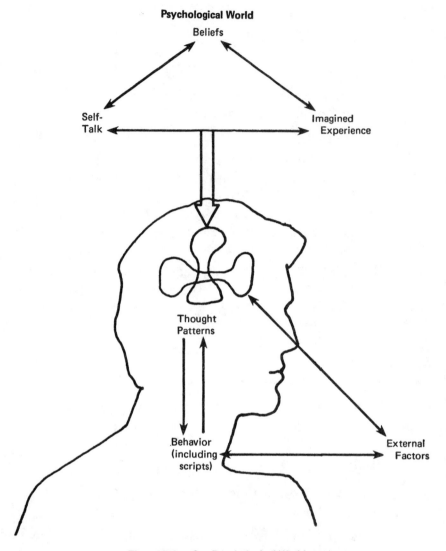

Figure 5-3. Our Psychological Worlds

our thought patterns. Of course, these factors are influenced by external forces such as our past experiences. The primary idea, however, is that we each construct a unique concept of life in our minds that influences our actions and how we feel about things.

Notice also that in Figure 5-3 behavior is included as both an influence and a result of our thought patterns. There has been considerable debate and controversy recently over, essentially, a "chicken-or-egg" issue: Does our psychological makeup (e.g., attitudes, beliefs) cause our behavior, or does our behavior cause our psychological makeup? The logical answer is a bit facetious, "yes"; that is, they cause each other. Thus, an optimal approach to improving our self-leadership includes a focus on both. Indeed, there is considerable evidence that if we change our behavior we change ourselves psychologically. If we behave in a more courteous and friendly manner toward others, we are likely to change psychologically into more courteous and friendly people. Because of the strong interrelationship of our behavior and our thoughts, it is useful at this point to focus on an especially insightful view of behavior. This view centers around the concept of behavioral scripts.

Behavioral scripts.[9] The work that has been done concerning behavioral scripts suggests that we tend to adopt stereotyped sequences of behaviors that we use when faced with certain types of situations. For example, when entertaining dinner guests in our home we act out certain expected sequences of behaviors such as taking their coats, asking them to sit down and make themselves at home, offering them something to drink before dinner, and the like. We could easily identify many other occasions that call for specific scripts for us to act out (eating at a restaurant, attending church, attending a formal business meeting). The idea of scripts suggests that we automatically tend to behave in certain ways when cued to do so by a particular situation. Thus, attempts to change our behavior, either as a result of or as a means of changing our thought patterns, should recognize the important role played by scripts. Scripts might be thought of as the machinery that drives much of our learned behavior. To improve our behavior may require the development of new, more desirable scripts.

The development of new, more desirable scripts requires a greater awareness of our current script "library" (the repertoire of scripts that we call upon and act out in different situations). By paying attention to our current habitual behavioral performances in different situations, we can obtain a better understanding of why we behave as we do. Also, by identifying scripts that we believe would be more effective in these different situations and by rehearsing them and reinforcing ourselves for using them we can increase our personal effectiveness.

The ideas presented in this chapter, however, would suggest that dealing with the physical, observable aspects of our behavioral scripts is not enough. That is, our efforts to improve on our scripted behavior will likely require that we go beyond the physical and observable level to an inner psychological level. Indeed, thought patterns stemming from habitual self-statements and imagined experiences (mental behavior) could be thought of as psychological scripts. When faced with a difficult interpersonal situation calling for assertiveness (such as a disagreement, for example), if we tend habitually to experience certain destructive self-statements ("You're in over your head"; "You'd better give him his way") and images of the worst (embarrassment and failure if we continue to attempt to express our view), we have, in essence, developed a dysfunctional psychological script. Our dysfunctional psychological script, in turn, is likely to lead to dysfunctional scripted physical behavior as well (giving in even though we know we are right). The point is that we tend to develop scripts to deal with certain types of recurring situations. These scripts can exist at a physical level, a psychological level, or a combination of the two.

Improving our thought patterns is indeed an important aspect of enhancement of our personal effectiveness. The relationship between our pattern of thinking and our behavior, however, will often call for more than thinking our way to new isolated behaviors. In many cases it may call for changing entire sequences of deep-rooted stereotypical behaviors (both physical and psychological) that have been habitually matched to specific situations. What behavioral sequences do you have stored in your current script "library"? Do you think you could identify and learn more desirable scripts to call upon when faced with different acts or scenes in the ultimate theatrical event: life?

A checklist designed to help you adopt the scripts that you believe are most effective follows. Also, a short exercise to help you apply these ideas to your own "real-world" theatrical parts is provided

Adopting "New Improved" Scripts Exercise

Adopt new, more desirable scripts. Follow the steps below.

1. Identify some important, specific types of situations that you face on a recurring basis that especially evoke your acting out an automatic sequence of behaviors and thoughts (a script).

2. Analyze your scripts. How do your scripts in the situations identified in step 1 affect your performance and your results? Which scripts do you think are ineffective that you would like to eliminate from your script "library"?

3. Create some new, more desirable scripts to take the place of your ineffective ones. What combinations and sequences of behaviors do you think would be especially effective for dealing with the recurrent situations you identified in step 1?

4. Practice your new scripts. First, rehearse privately the new sequences of behaviors and thoughts that you identified previously. Then, use the scripts when faced with actual situations that are appropriate for a particular script. Make notes about your progress in actual situations (use a form similar in format to the following).

Situation _Nature of the script used_ _Results and suggested improvements_

5. Use self-leadership to manage your progress. Use _self-observation_ to assess your progress (as suggested by the format for keeping notes in step 4). Use _self-reward_ when you successfully perform effective scripts in the specific situations identified in the form. Also, use the other self-leadership techniques that you find helpful to remind you of the specific behaviors included in your new scripts.

Checklist for Creating
"New Improved" Scripts for Your Life Situations

☐ Learn and use "new improved" scripts

  ☐ Study your current script "library"—what kinds of habitual behavioral sequences do you act out when faced with important situations? What kinds of images and self-statements do you habitually draw upon in response to these situations?

  ☐ Identify scripts that are undesirable that you would like to eliminate (both in your physical behavior and your thoughts)

  ☐ Create new, more desirable scripts to take the place of your ineffective ones

  ☐ Rehearse your new scripts—mentally and physically work through and practice the behavioral and psychological sequences you would like to adopt

  ☐ Use your new scripts when faced with appropriate situations—exercise self-leadership in adopting new scripts. For example:

    • Use self-observation to assess your progress and make further improvements

    • Reward yourself for successfully performing your new improved scripts

  ☐

  ☐

In conclusion, even though this chapter has focused on our thinking as a means of changing our psychological worlds, we must not forget the perhaps less direct yet very important influence of behavior. For example, if we want to change in some way (e.g., become more assertive) and if we behave in a consistent manner with this goal (e.g., behave more assertively), we increase our chances of achieving this end. Furthermore, such behavioral changes will often call for alteration of entire sequences of behavior (e.g., developing an assertive script). Of course, if we accept the idea of mental behavior (i.e., a thought is a mental behavior), then our focus is always on behavior, either mental or physical. By changing either type of behavior, we have the potential of changing ourselves.

To illustrate how our thought patterns can influence our thinking and our actions, I present the following example.

OPPORTUNITY OR OBSTACLE THINKING: AN EXAMPLE

Two types of thought patterns that a person could adopt are what might be called opportunity thinking and obstacle thinking. Opportunity thinking involves a pattern of thoughts that focus on the opportunities and possibilities that situations or challenges hold. Creative, innovative individuals who contribute to the major breakthroughs and advances in our world most likely possess this sort of pattern of thinking. Their beliefs, their imagined future experiences, and their self-talk probably spur them on to undertake new opportunities. Obstacle thinking, on the other hand, involves a focus on the roadblocks and pitfalls of undertaking new ventures. Such a mental pattern fosters avoidance of challenges in favor of more secure actions, often with substantially lesser potential payoffs.

Of course, each of us can possess both of these types of thought patterns at different times and when faced with different situations. There are undertakings that pose too much personal risk and that should be avoided. On the other hand, we often find ourselves caught up in difficult situations unexpectedly. Because avoiding the situation is no longer a choice, the issue becomes one of how to deal with it. We probably tend to rely on certain thought patterns more than others in dealing with life's challenges, as, for example, the following: thoughts that we should seek out worthwhile challenges because they help us grow, on the one hand, or thoughts that we should do our best to avoid as much as possible problems of any kind, on the other; thoughts that the world is cruel and unfair, on the one hand, or thoughts that the world is basically good and that honest effort is rewarded, on the other, and so forth. The pattern that our thinking takes influences our actions (e.g., our automatic performance of certain scripts), our satisfaction with life, and our personal effectiveness.

Let us return to the example of the thought patterns we have labeled *opportunity thinking* and *obstacle thinking*. Consider for a moment the dilemma posed by the world's growing energy short-age. One view concerning this problem is that we should focus on conserving what energy reserves we have left. This view suggests that we deal with the problem by reducing our consumption of energy to postpone the ultimate exhaustion of our resources as long as possible. The focus is primarily on the obstacles posed by the pressing problem. Another view suggests that unlimited energy is available and that we need only to identify and tap into it. Whether it is to be found in synthetics, in the splitting of atoms, in nature's sun and wind, or in some other source, the view would suggest that it is there to be discovered. In essence, the view might argue that if we can conceive of it, it can be found. Perhaps the most fruitful position would include both views. The point is, however, that the beliefs we hold about the dangers and possibilities involved, what we can imagine in our minds as a likely result of our efforts, and what we tell ourselves about the problem will influence our stand and the actions we take. Our viewpoints, too, can be self-fulfilling because the actions we take can create the physical reality. If we do not believe the discovery of safe, affordable energy alternatives is possible, our resulting inaction can confirm our thinking. Of course, the opposite effect can be achieved from a different pattern of thinking and action. Consider this example:

On March 30, 1981, then President Ronald Reagan was wounded in the chest by a would-be assassin's bullet. The horror of the situation was a shock to millions around the world. Logically, one would think President Reagan would condemn the violent act and display a negative outlook in the wake of the atrocity. Instead, the president was said to have smiled through surgery. Numerous optimistic and humorous quotes from the president reached the public, which gradually helped relieve the mass tension. The victim seemed to be trying to support the safe onlookers rather than the seemingly more logical reverse. "Honey, I forgot to duck" (to his wife); "Please, say you're Republicans" (to the doctors); the at-tempted assassination "ruined one of my best suits" (to his daugh-ter); "send me to L.A., where I can see the air I'm breathing" (to the medical staff) were among the verbal or written remarks of the wounded president.

The results? The president's popularity rose to an apparent all-time high. Momentum seemed to be given to the programs he had been working hard to push through Congress. A short time after the incident, the president achieved his first major political triumph since taking office—Congress approved his budget. This triumph could be attributed largely to his admirable conduct in the wake of the assassination attempt.[10]

Whether you are in agreement or not with this President's political views or his subsequent actions in office, it is difficult to deny that his reaction to this life-threatening assault is little short of amazing. The would-be tragedy seemed to have been transformed into a powerful opportunity. The public feeling surrounding this distressful event and the President's inspiring behavior is reflected in a view expressed by one television commentator. In essence he said, "I hope President Reagan feels better because of how bad we feel. I know how I feel. I wish I would have voted for him." Indeed, there may be opportunities in even the most unlikely of situations if only we let ourselves see them through the patterns of our thinking.

This idea is exemplified by the following composite example based on the experiences of participants in my training seminars and MBA classes.

The Case of the Problem Employee That Was All in Her Mind

Alicia Smith was a department manager for ABC Corporation. She was generally very good with her department employees, and her department consistently turned out solid performance. Recently, however, she had developed a poor relationship with one of her newer subordinates, Tim Williams. Unlike Alicia's other employees, Tim frequently questioned the instructions that Alicia provided for him. On a couple of occasions he had even questioned some of Alicia's ideas during department meetings in front of the other employees. Alicia had become particularly frustrated with the situation and was convinced that Tim was intentionally trying to undermine her authority. She felt that he was going to have a disruptive influence on other employees and on the department's overall performance.

Alicia was having lunch with a friend and peer, Dave Sims, the manager of another department in the company. "I don't know whether to recommend he be terminated, transferred, or if I should take formal disciplinary action toward him or what," Alicia was saying in a frustrated tone. "I just know its got to stop. I will not put up with it anymore," Alicia finished with emphasis.

"What exactly is he saying and doing?" Dave asked in a calm voice that didn't sound quite sympathetic enough to satisfy Alicia. "Is he being rude or behaving unethically or anything? Is he showing a lack of respect or refusing to do his work?"

"Well, no; not exactly," Alicia responded, looking at Dave a little suspiciously. "It's just that he's always arguing for another way of doing things as opposed to accepting my directions. In the end he does what I ask him to do and he works pretty hard at it but he seems to resent my authority, or at least he's hesitant to accept it without putting up a fight first."

"Oh, this sounds familiar. I've had a few workers who have acted in a similar way over the years. I used to think they were fighting me, too. Don't take this the wrong way, but what I finally realized was that usually I was fighting them, not the other way around. I misunderstood the situation."

He paused and studied Alicia to see how she was taking his comments. After deciding she looked hesitant but interested, he continued. "You see I learned through some reading and seminars I attended that we often make false assumptions and tell ourselves inaccurate things about difficult situations. After studying my situation I realized that frequently the employees who seemed to challenge me were actually trying to contribute more than I was asking of them. They were also trying to contribute their own ideas and insights. And usually I found that if I let them think of their own ways of doing things they ended up very committed to their work and very grateful and supportive of me for having the opportunity to really contribute."

Dave proceeded to describe to Alicia a system he developed for challenging his own assumptions and self-statements to help him more constructively deal with difficult situations like relating to what appear to be problem subordinates. He also used visualization techniques to mentally rehearse and imagine constructive ways of dealing with his challenges. He explained: "Some of those difficult people who seem like major obstacles to performance actually represent tremendous opportunities if you can just help them constructively channel their energy and creativity."

Over another couple of lunches and a couple of short meetings, Dave helped Alicia to understand and apply the important parts of his personal thought management system in a way that seemed most appealing and useful to her. Almost immediately she noticed improvements in her relationship with Tim. She began to see that Tim was in fact trying to contribute what he viewed as better ways of reaching high performance in his work. As Alicia began to allow Tim to pursue more of his own ideas, she was pleased to observe that many of his ideas did pay off with significant results. Sometimes he did make mistakes but he worked hard to correct them. Most of all, Tim became a highly committed employee and one of Alicia's strongest supporters and performers.

As an additional benefit, Alicia gradually found increased satisfaction in her own job as she learned to constructively manage her assumptions and self-statements about troubling situations. She also worked on the mental images she pictured about challenging situations and worked to make sure that they were constructive. Over time her employees developed a reputation for being some of the most creative and committed people in the company. Alicia no longer viewed challenging employees as personal threats but as positive opportunities. As a consequence, that's just what they became.

Spend some time thinking about how you think. What are your overall thinking habits? What kind of patterns do your beliefs, imagined experiences, and self-talk create in your thinking? Are the scripts you act out effective? Do they enhance your psychological world and your performance? Do you tend to search for the opportunities or do you tend to search for obstacles in challenges? What kind of thought patterns would you like to establish in your mind? How can you adapt your beliefs, imagined experiences, self-talk, and your behavior to establish these patterns? The time you spend now sorting through questions such as these may make all the difference in how you spend your life.

ENDNOTES

[1] See, for example, Albert Ellis, *A New Guide to Rational Living* (Englewood Cliffs, N.J.: Prentice Hall, 1975; and Albert Ellis and John M. Whiteley, (eds.), *Theoretical and Empirical Foundations of Rational Emotive Therapy* (Monterey, Calif: Brooks/Cole, 1979).

[2] Norman Vincent Peale, *The Power of Positive Thinking*, (New York: Spire Books, 1956).

[3] Norman Vincent Peale, *The Amazing Results of Positive Thinking*, (New York: Fawcett Crest Books, 1959).

[4] Daniel Goleman, "Research Affirms Power of Positive Thinking," *New York Times*, February 3, 1987, p. 15N.

[5] Ellis, *A New Guide to Rational Living*; and Ellis and Whiteley, *Theoretical and Empirical Foundations*. See also David Burns, *Feeling Good: The New Mood Therapy*, (New York: Morrow, 1980).

[6]Donald Meichenbaum and Roy Cameron, "The Clinical Potential of Modifying What Clients Say to Themselves," in M. J. Mahoney and C. E. Thoresen (eds.), *Self-Control: Power to the Person* (Monterey, Calif.: Brooks/Cole, 1974).

[7]For an interesting treatment of a number of strategies for effectively using self-talk, see Shad Helmstetter, *What to Say When You Talk to Yourself* (New York: Pocket Books, 1986).

[8]Meichenbaum and Cameron, "The Clinical Potential."

[9]For information on scripts, see Robert P. Abelson, "Psychological Status of the Script Concept," *American Psychologist*, 36 (1981), 715–729; and Dennis A. Gioia and Charles C. Manz, "Linking Cognition and Behavior: A Script Processing Interpretation of Vicarious Learning, *Academy of Management Review*, 10 (1985), 527–539.

[10]Ed Magnuson (reported by L. I. Barrett and N. MacNeil), "Reagan's Big Win," *Time*, May 18, 1981, pp.14–16.

6

Reviewing Travel Tales of Previous Journeys

or

Examples of Self-Leadership in Practice

A miracle is the occurrence of a natural event that we did not know (or let ourselves believe) was possible.

The ultimate journey is the discovery of the vast potential (the miracles) locked in each one of us.

Many examples of applications of the self-leadership ideas brought together in this book are available. An attempt will be made here to present some of these examples. Hundreds of participants in my training workshops and college courses have applied strategies presented in this book to their own problems and challenges according to their own self-designed plans. These many experiences formed the basis for many of the examples shared throughout. The purpose of this chapter is to provide further real-life support for the argument that self-leadership techniques and strategies offer many potential benefits when effectively and systematically practiced. The discussion will touch briefly on three categories of self-leadership application: (1) personal problems, (2) athletics, and (3) organizational/work problems. Applications to personal problems and athletics will be briefly discussed before addressing the primary focus of this book: organizational/work challenges. Hopefully, the combination of these different types of application will provide a better picture of the wide applicability and potential of self-leadership strategies.

SELF-LEADERSHIP APPLIED TO PERSONAL PROBLEMS

Probably the most extensive application of systematic, self-regulatory strategies has occurred in the field of psychology.[1] More specifically, major strides have been made in developing the ability of individuals to deal more effectively with their own problems. Specific difficulties that have been addressed are too numerous to discuss fully here. Instead, a brief comment will be made on a sampling of self-leadership applications to personal problems. It is useful to look at these examples first because much of the idea development that is included in this book can ultimately be traced to psychology-based applications to personal problems.

Consider the challenge of controlling eating behavior when confronted with an overweight problem. Various strategies have been applied, many with impressive success, to deal with this difficulty. One of the original approaches, for example, involved various cueing strategies. The logic employed was that many dysfunctional eating behaviors stem from personal exposure to dysfunctional cues in our environment. Since cues such as watching television, reading, and socializing often become associated with eating, one way of controlling eating is to control these cues. Thus, numerous individuals have benefited (lost substantial weight) by restricting their eating to only a limited number of infrequent situations (e.g., dinner time) and purposefully not eating in other situations that could potentially become a cue to future eating (watching television).

Similar techniques have also been applied to smoking behavior, with significant success (in reducing smoking) in many cases. One particularly interesting example employed the use of a specially designated smoking chair that was located in unpleasant surroundings (e.g., the garage). By limiting smoking only to this chair, many other potential cues (e.g., watching television, drinking a cup of coffee at the dinner table) for smoking behavior are eliminated.

Many other self-regulatory strategies have been applied to these dysfunctional, habitual behaviors. By altering self-statements regarding weight loss (e.g., "I've been torturing myself with starvation and I'm just not losing much weight," to "I'm making progress. I'm losing pounds slowly but surely"), many individuals have reported beneficial results. Similarly, self-reinforcement for improving eating habits has been of significant help to weight losers. A nice dinner out (nutritionally balanced, of course) as a reward for achieving a weight loss goal (e.g., losing 10 pounds) can provide incentive for future weight loss. Treatment of eating and smoking problems has also used various forms of imagery (e.g., imagining negative results such as excessive weight problems or cancer) associated with the focal behavior to promote beneficial results.

One particularly interesting application of imagined experience has been made to a type of interpersonal behavior—assertiveness.[2] Specifically, individuals were instructed to imagine scenes that called for them to be assertive and to imagine positive results from their assertive behavior. Individuals might imagine themselves in a restaurant, for example, receiving a steak cooked medium-well when they ordered it medium-rare. They would then imagine themselves sending the steak back and asking to receive another one cooked as they ordered it (medium-rare). Finally, they would imagine receiving an excellent steak just as they wanted, and receiving other positive results (such as the manager making a reduction to the total amount on their check because of their inconvenience) stemming from their assertiveness. Systematic use of imagery, such as that described, over a period of time was found to benefit many individuals by helping them to increase significantly their subsequent assertiveness.

APPLICATIONS IN ATHLETICS

Many self-leadership techniques have also been applied, in various forms, to athletics. Reflecting this emphasis, several articles (combined into a special feature focusing on the psychological and social aspects of physical activity) were published in an issue of the *Journal of Physical Education, Recreation and Dance* (March, 1982). Interestingly, the material presented in these articles closely parallels several of the major themes of this book. (The material emphasizes strategies such as self-observation, self-goal-setting, and rehearsal; it focuses directly on important behaviors; it addresses the importance of natural enjoyment of activities derived from feelings of competence and personal control; and it argues for the importance of thought patterns established through effective use of imagery, self-talk, and essentially positive, or opportunity, thinking.)

A comprehensive review of the extensive applications of self-leadership strategies to athletic activity is beyond the scope of this book. Indeed, a growing area known as *sport psychology* has provided much knowledge on the subject. It is instructive, however, to review some particularly interesting examples for illustrative purposes. The use of self-set goals is one strategy that is especially relevant to athletics. Whether the goal involves field-goal percentage for a basketball player, running the mile in a specific time for a runner, or achieving a specified score for 18 holes of golf, self-goal-setting can provide an athlete with direction for his or her efforts. Some athletes set goals that are too high, however, so that they cannot possibly achieve them. It is important that goals be challenging, but achievable.

For athletes this frequently means that the focus needs to be on process-related goals such as effort, form, and strategy rather than the outcome of a contest. In young soccer players, for example, evidence has been found that stress, which can undermine the natural enjoyment of a recreational activity, results from individual perceptions of an inability to meet performance demands.[3] Obviously, since competition usually means that some one or team has to lose (and usually that means 50 percent of those participating), goals focusing on winning may not be particularly effective. In many cases an athlete may do his or her best, but simply does not possess the ability to beat an outstanding opponent.

An especially intriguing area of self-leadership application to athletics centers on the creative use of imagery to facilitate desirable performance. A review of 60 different sports studies, across a wide range of activities and ages of performers, found a consistent positive relationship between constructive mental imagery and performance.[4] For example, one author commented on a highly successful golf instructor and a well-known professional golfer who both strongly advocated that players should picture the ideal golf swing in their mind to improve their game.[5] The logic employed is that if players can imagine themselves smoothly and cleanly performing a golf shot that accomplishes what they want it to (and they do this before actually swinging), the result is likely to be a more natural and effective shot.

A similar process has been used in many other sports as well. Reports have been made of Olympic gymnasts, for example, who employ imagery as an aid to performance.[6] One gymnast said that before an event she imagines what she sees when she actually performs. Another explained that she feels the motion in her muscles as though actually performing. Likewise, at least one world class high jumper has employed imagery: If he could mentally picture himself slowly floating over the bar, he knew he could make the jump. A highly successful swimming team at a major state university employs imagined experience as part of its preparation for competition. Swimmers are encouraged to imagine the race, including the feeling of the water on their bodies, their strokes, breathing, and so forth before the race begins.

Interestingly, before I was aware of the systematic application of imagery to athletics, I had often used imagery in my own recreational activity. In high school, for example, I competed in varsity wrestling, football, and track. Before a wrestling match I often mentally pictured just what I intended to do—in many cases right down to the pinning hold. Frequently I was able to carry out much of what I had imagined in actual performance. Similarly, before a track event I would imagine my strategy for the race, such as when I would start pouring on extra speed, whether I would save some strength for a sprint at the end, and so forth. These mental images were often so real that I would find myself using muscles and shifting my weight according to the physical demands required in the mental image.

Also, the overall pattern of thinking that an athlete brings to a sport appears to be especially important. Terms that are frequently used in reference to competitions, such as getting "psyched up" or being "psyched out," reflect the importance many place on this critical role. The need for athletes to believe in their ability to perform and to engage in facilitative rather than destructive thoughts may be in many cases as important as physical practice and preparation. The idea of "psychological barriers" to performance in athletics is an interesting example.[7] The four-minute mile, the seven-foot-high jump, and the eighteen-foot pole vault are examples of the obstacles to athletic achievement that are as much psychologically as physically based. Interestingly, some evidence exists suggesting that if weight lifters are deceived into believing that they are lifting less weight than they actually are, this psychological belief enables them to lift significantly more weight than they could otherwise.[8] The need for athletes to focus on the positive aspects of an event and to engage in constructive rather than destructive self-statements (e.g., "I've practiced hard and I can do well," rather than "I hope I don't blow it; I'm just not sure I can do it") has been emphasized.[9] Remember that, according to Roger Banister (the first man to run the mile in less than four minutes), a major reason why so many have now run under a four-minute mile is because runners finally came to *believe* that it could be done.

APPLICATIONS IN WORK/ORGANIZATIONAL SITUATIONS

Systematic attempts to apply self-leadership methods to work organizations are still at a relatively early stage of development. Nonetheless, examples of innovative applications are available that indicate a great deal of promise. These examples can be found across a wide range of organizational positions, including uniquely autonomous jobs that are particularly suited for and in need of self-leadership (e.g., salespersons, dentists, and medical doctors, college professors), managers in organizations, and non-management workers. Some of these applications will be discussed briefly in order to reflect the progress that has been made, as well as the vast potential for the future.

UNIQUELY AUTONOMOUS JOBS

Uniquely autonomous jobs in organizations are of special interest for self-leadership. Certainly salespersons who spend a great deal of time traveling by themselves and calling on customers find that to a large degree they must be their own managers. Training in sales techniques and an expression of confidence in their abilities by the home office are often not enough for many to handle this challenge successfully. In the short run, for example, treating themselves to an expensive dinner with wine for closing a big sale may be the only material reward they receive until returning home from a trip in the field. Salespersons need to play a critical role in their own development, motivation, and systematic self-leadership. Setting personal goals, rehearsing sales presentations, administering self-rewards, and seeking out the natural rewards in their job could mean the difference between success and failure.

Indeed, many other jobs present similar challenges—from the loosely supervised machine operator on a midnight shift to the chief executive officer of a large corporation who has ultimate authority for the direction of a business. My own line of work, a college professor and consultant, demands a high level of self-leadership. Yet my experience has revealed numerous cases in my profession in which individuals (including myself) have had personal and professional setbacks because of ineffective self-leadership practice. These setbacks often result from setting unrealistic goals, being overly self-critical, and engaging in dysfunctional thought patterns (e.g., inaccurate, debilitating, imagined experiences relating to immediate behavior choices).

In order to explore more fully the role of self-leadership for individuals who are in highly autonomous positions, one especially challenging type of job will be singled out as an example—namely, the entrepreneur. For our purposes, an entrepreneur can be described as an owner-manager of a firm who sets its course and largely determines its fate: success or failure. Entrepreneurs are in a difficult position, since they must, largely on their own, beat the staggering odds against new business ventures. (It has been estimated that as few as 1 out of 100 survive three years.) A colleague, Dr. Charles Snyder, and I have conducted a series of personal interviews with several successful entrepreneurs (i.e., those who have survived, against all odds, longer than three years and were currently doing well) operating a wide range of businesses.[10] We found that, although they may play down the use of any systematic management strategies on their part, they displayed several common threads of a systematic self-leadership fabric in their behavior. A few of the self-leadership applications they revealed to us follow.

Consider Mr. Air (the name is changed, of course, to protect confidentiality), the majority stock owner and manager of a commuter airline in the southern United States. Mr. Air uses the strategy of self-observation, for example, by keeping a daily log (a detailed record of how he spends his time). He also keeps a record of what he says to others over the phone regarding business matters in order to help him be consistent in his future dealings with these people. Mr. Air has adopted various cueing strategies to help manage himself. He uses a chalkboard directly in front of his desk, for example, to record notes that serve as a reminder and a guide for his work efforts. He also makes use of both self-applied and natural rewards. He enjoys reviewing his performance and feeling good about (he mentally rewards himself for) his achievements and, in general, just seems to get a kick out of (experiences the natural rewards of) what he is doing. (He even continues to exercise his pilot's prerogative by taking a turn at flying some of the airline's routes.)

Perhaps the most striking feature of Mr. Air's approach to his work is his eye to opportunities. Many of his competitors have gone out of business, yet he is determined to expand to take advantage of new opportunities rather than reduce services. In fact, shortly before our interview, Mr. Air had worked out a creative financial plan, despite low funds, to buy a larger airplane. He was quite exuberant, and rightly so, as he told us of this accomplishment. He didn't need us to tell him that this was quite an achievement—it was apparent from the satisfied expression on his face and the energetic tone of his voice that he had already taken care of that himself. As he put it, "Self-gratification—that's what it's all about."

Mr. Air is just one of many successful entrepreneurs who, although seeming to be unaware that they are doing so, reveals obvious signs of systematic self-leadership practice. Consider Mr. Notes, the owner-manager of a successful company in the Midwest that distributes synopses of college textbooks. He relies heavily on self-set goals to help him direct his own behavior and facilitate the success of his business. Particularly in the early days of his business, he found goals to be invaluable in directing his efforts toward the development of his company and to serve as a basis for exercising another self-leadership strategy—self-reward. More specifically, Mr. Notes has found providing monetary bonuses for himself contingent on achieving sales goals to be an effective strategy for facilitating his performance.

Mr. Restaurant (the owner of a small family restaurant), on the other hand, found posting checklists (a cueing strategy) to be a useful method of ensuring that he, as well as other employees, consistently follow established procedures and maintain acceptable levels of performance. In addition, when important performance goals are achieved, Mr. Restaurant and his employees close up and throw a party for themselves.

Mr. Sport, the owner-manager of a sporting goods store, combines the strategies of self-goal-setting and self-observation to manage himself. He sets two-year goals and records them on a checklist (a self-observation strategy), enabling him to make additions and deletions and keep track of delays in goal attainment. He is always searching for new goals, and frequently breaks longer-term goals into more immediate targets for his daily efforts. Mr. Sport also reported an especially powerful self-reward process that helps him maintain his motivation. As he accomplishes goals and reviews his own performance favorably, he feels a "rush of adrenaline" and experiences a "terrific high." Indeed, Mr. Sport appears to be positively urged onward by a combination of internal self-praise and the natural rewards of succeeding on the job.

ORGANIZATIONAL MANAGEMENT POSITIONS

Managers are well suited for systematic self-leadership practice. Organizational research, as well as personal experience and observation, has made me acutely aware of the difficult challenges that require managers to be especially good self-managers. If they are not, they can easily become poor managers of others and of organizational resources. For many, the fast-paced, multifaceted demands of a management position can become overwhelming. As phones ring off the hook, subordinates wait for their attention, multiple deadlines stare them in the face, a seemingly endless onslaught of meetings compete for their time, and they are snowed under by a mountain of information and "urgent" demands, the potential for ineffectiveness and inefficiency is enormous. Peter Drucker has described effectiveness as "doing the right thing," and efficiency as "doing things right."[11] In essence, a manager—despite typically being in a sizable organization that imposes guidelines, constraints, and offers various incentives—must largely choose among his vast demands, what he will spend his time on, and how he will expend his effort on the tasks he chooses to deal with. Self-leadership practices of managers can be instrumental in determining if they are doing the right things and doing them correctly.

    Some interesting applications of self-leadership strategies have been successfully employed by several managers and have been reported in some interesting recent research.[12] These applications involved managers in a variety of jobs in retailing, manufacturing, public service, and advertising, including both line and staff positions. In the various cases reported, specific behaviors were identified (e.g., time spent on the phone, timely completion of expense forms, informing others when leaving the office) for improvement, appropriate to the individual manager involved.

The advertising manager of a newspaper, for example, was able to deal effectively with several behaviors he identified as needing improvement. One problem targeted was his tendency to leave the office without leaving word where he was going and when he would be back that day (if at all). A simple cueing strategy was used to solve the problem: A "checkout" board was placed on the office door which he could not miss seeing when leaving. Magnetic disks on the board could easily be moved to indicate if he was out of the building, if he would return, and when.

Similarly, a problem he had in getting himself to fill out expense forms on a timely basis (neglected sometimes for several months) was eliminated by having a secretary place an appropriate form on his desk at an appropriate time of the day (in the evening just before he went home). He always tried to be back in the office just before leaving for home, and usually did not have many demands placed on him at this time. Thus, he could easily complete this task when cued by the form on his desk to do so. In addition, a wall chart was placed on his wall for the purposes of self-observation—soon the manager was filling out the form every day. The wall chart, which indicated this performance improvement, provided the occasion for self-reinforcement. Also, by properly filling out the expense forms, the manager received the added benefits of not incurring personal financial loss (from not being timely reimbursed for his expenses) and was able to get a more accurate picture of expenses in his department.

In another case an assistant retail store manager identified a behavior she would like to improve: frequent visits to her boss, resulting in excessive dependence (her boss agreed that this was detracting from her effectiveness). To deal with the problem, she used a simple self-observation strategy—she would carry an index card on which she recorded the frequency of her visits, the type of information she wanted at the time, and what happened when she handled the problem herself rather than consulting her boss. Subsequently, the frequency of her visits reduced drastically, and both she and her boss were pleased with her performance.

In addition to these case studies, I have conducted considerable research on this topic both for individuals in more traditional work environments and more contemporary participative and team-based environments.[13] I have also observed numerous instances that provide insight regarding self-management of managers. I have witnessed, as you probably have, many instances where managers have developed their own tailor-made self-leadership strategies to deal with behaviors needing improvement. I have seen countless managers use checklists to guide their daily behaviors. I have seen managers take coffee breaks after successfully completing important tasks, or switch their attention to a more enjoyable activity as a reward for their accomplishment. I have seen managers turn routine tasks into a kind of game or competition to make their work more naturally rewarding. I am also familiar with managers who have visualized the potential rewards of successfully handling current challenges (recognition, promotion, or imagining the achievement of some of the dreams they have regarding their work).

Unfortunately, I have also seen managers mentally and physically beaten by the way they approached their work. One manager, for example, reported extreme worry associated with his work. His thoughts seemed always occupied by images of impending disaster on the job—failure, reprimand from his boss, humiliation resulting from poor performance, and even dismissal. The pressures associated with his job (most of which were apparently greatly exacerbated in his mind, he admitted) made him irritable at work and at home, very dissatisfied with his job, and brought him significant physical problems. He reported difficulty in sleeping, and exhibited excessive tension that was sometimes debilitating to the point of making him physically ill. The pattern of his physical and mental behavior may well be bringing him to other more serious problems, such as ulcers or perhaps worse: One of his associates had recently had his second heart attack, apparently brought on by "overpressing" at work.

I am also familiar with another manager who worked in the same organization. He, in contrast, was very enthusiastic about his work and seemed to be quite well adjusted. He practiced several self-leadership strategies (he was especially sold on "time management" techniques) and was well organized, relying heavily on systematic analysis of business information. In particular, he had a strong sense of task completion. Until he achieved immediate goals, he was persistent in his work efforts. In many ways he seemed like the model contemporary manager.

Unfortunately, this individual's strong sense of self-leadership did not extend to his impact on his environment or, more specifically, his immediate subordinates. His systematic approach to man-' agement was, frankly, not very palatable to his subordinates. They preferred to operate based on a "sense of the business" or intuition based on experience rather than to systematically gather data and fill out reports. Ultimately the friction came to a head and the manager was squeezed out of the organization—despite a solid performance record.

The case of the manager discussed above illustrates once again the complexity of self-leadership. Indeed, we must recognize the importance of the indirect impact of our actions on our external world (e.g., the work environment) as well as the direct way we manage our own behavior and thoughts. Unfortunately, our work environment is often very difficult to manage; for example, I have observed the frustrating plight of many managers attempting to maintain a consistent level of performance and motivation in the face of seemingly irrational organization roadblocks. I remember an instance when a customer wanted an odd table leaf owned by a large company—and the company wanted to get rid of the leaf that was taking up space. Unfortunately, the computer ticket that reported the style number, manufacturer, and other information for inventory purposes had become detached and lost. There was the customer, and there was the table leaf, but a manager in charge of the selling area could not for the life of him—despite numerous inquiries regarding appropriate procedures—figure out how to sell the leaf without breaking company policy for inventory control purposes.

I also remember a manager who had been assigned, essentially, one and one-half jobs: his usual tasks in addition to the large bulk of what another individual had previously worked on full time. A few months later, computer reports revealed that the business was up 70 percent over the previous year. Despite these improved figures, he received little, if any, positive feedback from his superiors. On the other hand, a short time later when some inventory had been temporarily misplaced (by persons working for advertising and display without his knowledge and permission), he was vigorously chewed out by a vice president. Similarly, concern was expressed when financial indicators showed performance had dropped temporarily to a mere 40 percent, rather than 70 percent, ahead of the previous year. Fortunately, he was able to maintain his performance level and reasonably good morale by recognizing and reinforcing himself in the absence of external recognition.

There was also the case of the manager who was considered somewhat ridiculous and was sometimes openly chided by peers because she refused to distort certain financial figures to make performance look better on paper than it really was. This was a commonly accepted practice in the organization, despite the fact that to an outsider it would probably appear rather unethical. This manager's sense of ethics (her own personal standards) conflicted directly with those of her peers. To maintain the personal stand she believed in, she had to exercise self-leadership influence in excess of the external forces she faced.

Managers face difficult challenges. With significant pressures and often inhospitable external work environments (not to mention the difficulty involved in trying to effectively manage one's self), achieving personal effectiveness can be difficult. While special problems such as the management of time or controlling stress have received specific attention, managing one's own day-to-day behavior has been largely neglected. This book is intended to be a significant first step in providing managers, and others, with practical tools for self-leadership. It represents a beginning step in dealing with challenges such as those discussed in this chapter.

NONMANAGEMENT JOBS

Lower-level, hourly-type jobs, the seemingly most unlikely focus for self-leadership application, have received perhaps the greatest attention. Recent growth in the adoption of "self-managed" or "autonomous" work teams in production/manufacturing plants as well as various other types of work settings (e.g., coal mines, warehouses, paper mills, and service organizations in insurance, financial services, and even psychiatric care) is the most striking example of this emphasis. The primary method I will use here to illustrate the need and potential of self-leadership methods for hourly workers is to draw upon examples from my personal experience and research. I have completed research projects in many self-managed team work systems across a wide variety of industries (both manufacturing and service) and work settings. In particular, I will place special emphasis on contrasting my personal experience as a machine operator in a "traditionally managed" manufacturing plant some years ago while a college student with more recent observations I obtained from a research project conducted in a manufacturing plant based on a self-managed team work system.

The plants were similar in numerous ways: Both used assembly-line technology, employed blue-collar workers with a relatively low level of education, and were even owned by the same corporation. A primary difference existed, however, regarding the way people were managed in the plant.

A common impression of blue-collar jobs in production/manufacturing plants is that they are monotonous, boring, and dehumanizing. My own experience did not contradict this impression. The extent to which people in such work settings have been typically underutilized is especially striking. I witnessed an interesting illustration of this tendency while working as a machine operator on a midnight shift. I had been operating a lathe, as did several other workers around me, for several nights. On this particular evening I was approached by the foreman. He expressed in some heated words that I was not producing enough output. Up to this time I had been attempting to work at about the same pace as other workers, being sensitive to productivity norms that assured workers of not making each other look bad. The foreman's comments, however, apparently hit a raw nerve concerning my need for achievement—and I began working "like crazy." Soon my output was noticeably increased on the conveyer line that wound its way through my part of the plant. A short time later the foreman approached me again, this time grinning. "Wow, you're really going now. Good job," he remarked.

Meanwhile, another worker nearby had been observing all this. He was a black man in his mid-thirties. He had always struck me as a particularly bright individual (though not well educated), but not very motivated. In fact, I had recently learned that he would press the production counter lever on his lathe (I later found out this was a common practice in the plant) to make it appear that his production was higher than it really was. He moved slowly and looked lazy.

On this occasion, however, he suddenly came to life. I remember being awed by the controlled speed and smoothness of his motions. He started "producing like hell," though with apparent lack of effort and fatigue. His face had come to life, as well, with determination and even pride. He was apparently trying to show the college punk a thing or two—and he did. I felt rather awkward and inadequate in comparison.

The funny thing about the episode is that soon it seemed as if it had never happened. A couple of days later I had fallen back to a more restricted level of production, assisted by various subtle pressures from other workers. Meanwhile, the "super" lathe operator returned to his normal behavior and he recaptured the dull, bored look on his face. He never produced the way he had that night during the remainder of my tenure in the plant.

Of course, workers suffering from a severe lack of motivation are not found only in manufacturing plants; unfortunately, they seem to be everywhere. Often the motivation that these workers do possess is much more oriented to avoiding work than to doing it. For example, I was familiar with one individual who worked in a warehouse who displayed an amazing aptitude in this regard. The creativity and effort he expended on avoiding work sometimes seemed to exceed that required to just go ahead and do the work. He seemed to enjoy avoiding his work so much more than doing it, so that's what he did.

Individuals such as this are not just lazy people without ambition. In fact, I have encountered many "work avoiders" who displayed obvious enthusiasm when they talked about their dreams of what they would *really* like to do. One factory worker I knew related to me with excitement the dream he planned to fulfill some day: It was to open a Disneyland-type of park for blacks. As he talked about it, the detail that he had worked out for his plan impressed me—the idea really sounded like it could work! Another, a warehouse worker, reported his ambition to own and operate his own ice cream parlor. The energy and enthusiasm he displayed as he talked about his dream was in sharp contrast to the dull lack of motivation he displayed on his current job. Indeed, people such as these do have a burning desire inside to put themselves into something they believe in. Unfortunately, at the time I knew them they seemed to lack the confidence and self-leadership capabilities to find a reasonable fit between their interests and their immediate and longer-term career efforts. They were wasting on their jobs.

One of the most striking examples of this sad state of affairs occurred on my last day of work on the midnight shift. I had become good friends with most people on the shift and was given a warm and hearty goodbye from many people. One of the workers (I'll call him Ed), however, was being conspicuously aloof. Since I had developed a particularly close tie with Ed and another worker on the shift, I was surprised at his behavior. He seemed rather depressed and perhaps a bit angry for some reason. I finally asked my other friend what the problem was. He explained that Ed was feeling really down because I was going back to college and he was stuck on a job he did not like. It seems that years earlier Ed had chosen to work at the plant because the money was good—he had always planned to get into some other "more rewarding" type of work. Now he was finally realizing that it was, perhaps, too late. He had become dependent on the money and his youth had been largely spent; he had led himself into what he now saw as the trap of many unmotivated, demoralized, American workers. This reality was dealing him a painful blow that evening. I have never seen him since, but I'll never forget the cold reality of the psychological defeat that showed on his face that night.

It is little wonder to me that we have severe productivity problems in the United States when I see workers such as these. They just don't derive any enjoyment in their work. Fortunately, it does not have to be that way. In fact, I have recently observed a situation in another manufacturing plant, this time as a researcher conducting a joint project with my colleague, Dr. Henry Sims, Jr., that supports this premise. What we saw was a sharp contrast to the examples I have related thus far. It was a plant that was organized on a self-managed team basis.[14] That is, production workers were provided with the autonomy and even the responsibility to do many things traditionally handled by managers (e.g., assigning group members to tasks, solving quality problems, and handling interpersonal problems between group members). Self-managed groups might be described as a step beyond the quality circles that have received so much attention because of their widespread use in Japan and extensive adoption in the United States. The important point for this discussion is that this plant, in contrast to the one I had worked in, allowed and even encouraged blue-collar workers to exercise self-leadership.

Perhaps a few examples will serve to illustrate the point. One case we observed involved a worker and his coordinator (in this plant supervisors were referred to as *coordinators* because of the unique aspects of the work system). The worker was asking his coordinator how he should go about repairing a guard rail on a loading ramp. The coordinator's response was essentially a question—"How do you think you should do it?" The worker responded by stating what he thought the appropriate solution was and, consistent with the nature of the work system, proceeded to act on his solution. He also seemed to do so with conviction and commitment that probably wouldn't have been there if he had been complying with an order. This case is not especially remarkable itself, but multiply this case many times and you have a situation that can only be described as amazing by comparison to the usual atmosphere found in most production plants today.

Some of our observations were much more striking. We witnessed one instance, for example, in which a worker apparently saved the plant a great deal of money.[15] He left his workstation to test some production materials he suspected were defective. He proceeded to a laboratory area, where he performed a test that proved he was right. After quite a bit of commotion in the plant, corrections were made that may have saved the plant a day or more of production and thousands of dollars. This same worker stayed after his shift hours without pay to help make the necessary corrections.

Having both worked in settings with climates more consistent with typical impressions of production plants—where employees are placed in monotonous jobs that turn people into unmotivated "machines" who don't care about productivity or quality—Dr. Sims and I were particularly amazed by instances such as these. We saw workers solve difficult technical and personal problems; we saw them volunteer to help complete difficult tasks without being told to do so; we heard them praise one another for work well done and provide negative feedback to fellow workers for not pulling their weight. We heard them refer to their work team's task responsibilities as "our business" and saw them talk to members of plant management (including the plant manager) as though they were equals. Most of all, we saw one of the best (and in many cases *the* best) plant in its product classification on many performance indicators measuring productivity, quality, safety, morale, turnover, and absenteeism.

The employees at the plant did not have the benefit of familiarity with the research and knowledge available regarding the systematic self-leadership strategies outlined in this book. Our research indicated, however, that they were already using many of these strategies without realizing they were doing so. The advantage they did have over workers in more traditional plants stemmed from their work environment, which provided the opportunity for them to use their innate abilities to lead themselves. This plant, we believe, represents just the tip of the iceberg in terms of what is possible. The primary stand of this book is that self-leadership can be used to improve one's own personal effectiveness. It can also be used, however, to help others become more effective. The manager who is wise enough to provide an environment for workers to exercise more fully their self-leadership potential, for example, could reap very substantial benefits on several bottom-line performance measures. In addition, by helping workers to master self-leadership skills (such as those outlined in this book), significant benefits should result for both the worker and the manager. All this calls for a new, more contemporary style of leadership—leadership that centers around the power of self-leadership.[16]

The tremendous potential of human beings to lead themselves to personal effectiveness is an expansive frontier just waiting to be explored. The examples related in this chapter are but a primitive glimpse of a few grains of the vast sands of self-leadership possibilities waiting to be tapped. Indeed, the ultimate journey is not the exploration of new lands or the outer regions of the cosmos; instead, it is the discovery of the tremendous unexplored regions of the human potential (the miracles) locked inside each one of us.

ENDNOTES

[1] See, for example, Carl E. Thoresen and Michael J. Machoney, *Behavioral Self-Control*, (New York: Holt, Rinehart and Winston, 1974; and Paul Karoly and Frederick H. Kanfer, eds., *Self-Management and Behavior Change* (New York: Pergamon Press, 1982).

[2] Alan E. Kazdin, "Effects of Covert Modeling and Model Reinforcement on Assertive Behavior," *Journal of Abnormal Psychology*, 83 (1974), 240–252; and Alan E. Kazdin, "Effects of Covert Modeling, Multiple Models, and Model Reinforcement on Assertive Behavior," *Behavior Therapy*, 7 (1976), 211–222.

[3] See T. K. Scanlon and M. W. Passer, "Sources of Competitive Stress in Young Female Athletes," *Journal of Sport Psychology*, 1 (1979), 151–159; and T. K. Scanlon and M. W. Passer, "Factors Restored to Competitive Stress Among Male Youth Sport Participants," *Medicine and Science in Sports*, 10 (1978), 276–281.

[4] D. L. Feltz and D. M. Landers, "The Effects of Mental Practice on Motor Skill Learning and Performance: A Meta-Analysis," *Journal of Sport Psychology*, 5 (1983), 25–57.

[5] Maxwell Maltz, *Psycho-Cybernetics* (Englewood Cliffs, N.J.: Prentice Hall, 1960), pp. 35–36.

[6] Michael J. Mahoney, "Cognitive Skills and Athletic Performance," in P. C. Kendall and S. D. Hollan (eds.), *Cognitive-Behavioral Intervention: Theory, Research, and Procedures* (New York: Academic Press, 1979).

[7] Ibid.

[8] R. G. Ness and R. W. Patton, "The Effects of Beliefs on Maximum Weight Lifting Performance," *Cognitive Theory and Research* (1980).

[9] See, for example, Debra L. Feltz and Maureen R. Weiss, "Developing Efficacy Through Sport," *Journal of Physical Education, Recreation and Dance* (March 1982), 24–26, 36.

[10] Charles C. Manz and Charles A. Snyder, "Entrepreneurial Self-Management or to Survive or Not to Survive, That Is the Question," *Management Review* (September 1983), 68–73.

[11] Peter F. Drucker, *Managing for Results* (New York: Harper & Row, 1964).

[12] Fred Luthans and Tim R. V. Davis, "Behavioral Self-Management—The Missing Link in Managerial Effectiveness," *Organizational Dynamics* (Summer 1979), 42–60.

[13] See, for example, Charles C. Manz and Henry P. Sims, Jr., "Leading Workers to Lead Themselves: The External Leadership of Self-Managing Work Teams," *Administrative Science Quarterly*, 32 (1987), 106–128.

[14] For a good description of some of the unique aspects of this plant, see Henry P. Sims, Jr., and Charles C. Manz, "Conversations with Autonomous Work Groups," *National Productivity Review* (Summer 1982), 261–269.

[15] Ibid.

[16] See, for example, Charles C. Manz and Henry P. Sims, Jr., *SuperLeadership: Leading Others to Lead Themselves* (Englewood Cliffs, N.J.: Prentice Hall, 1989; New York: Berkley [paperback], 1990).

7

The Destination
or
Self-Leadership

The end of a journey is the beginning of new opportunities.

The primary ingredients of the self-leadership framework presented in this book have now been introduced. In addition, Chapter 6 presented some examples indicating how specific self-leadership techniques have been used in several different types of real-life situations. The purpose of this chapter is to present an integrative self-leadership framework combining those elements that have been suggested thus far. An illustrative case will be offered that is designed to exemplify how the various self-leadership elements might be combined into a comprehensive self-leadership framework to develop a new, more effective way of working and living in our complex and often troublesome world.

It has been a long journey, but the destination and a beginning are at hand. Read on to see the full form of our ultimate goal: self-leadership.

SELF-LEADERSHIP

To gain a fuller understanding of self-leadership and the various factors involved, it is important to describe an integrative framework. In essence, we have thus far been focusing on and examining the details of the various pieces of a larger self-leadership puzzle.

At this point we will examine how these pieces fit together to form the complete picture.

Figure 7-1 presents a diagram combining the key elements discussed in previous chapters. Note that the three major parts of the diagram correspond with the topics of Chapters 3, 4, 5, and 6: strategies for doing unattractive but necessary tasks, tapping the power of natural rewards, and redesigning our psychological worlds. The primary strategies introduced for each of these three self-leadership perspectives are listed in an appropriate portion of the figure. Note that, consistent with Chapter 5, beliefs, imagined experiences, and self-talk are depicted as interacting factors which lead to the thought patterns that establish a unique psychological world for each of us. Also, the diagram points out that each of the three approaches to self-leadership influence and complement one another in forming a comprehensive framework.

Behavior is pictured at the center of the diagram which is the ultimate focus of self-leadership. That is, the primary concern of self-leadership is our behavior, mental (i.e., thoughts) as well as physical, and how it affects our personal effectiveness (our success in achieving our goals as well as our satisfaction with our work, ourselves, and our lives). The diagram points out that each of the three parts of self-leadership have an impact on our behavior and ultimately our personal effectiveness. Also, the important role of scripts in influencing behavior is indicated in the "Redesigning Your Psychological World" portion of the model. Both the direct effect of behavioral scripts and the indirect effect of psychological scripts are shown. The reciprocal influence between our behavior and our mode of thinking (our psychological world) is depicted as well by a two-directional arrow.

Figure 7-1 allows us to view the comprehensive systematic approach to self-leadership in its totality. A complex system of multiple variables is suggested, indicating that we have several points of departure in our undertaking to improve our self-leadership. Applying principles suggested by the various strategies that have been outlined should contribute to improvements in the other approaches as well. For example, by effectively applying self-leadership techniques (such as self-goal-setting and self-reward), indirect benefits, such as increased enjoyment of our work (natural rewards), and improved, more beneficial patterns of thought, should be fostered. Ultimately, beneficial application of the various techniques should contribute to a changed, more effective and rewarding life-

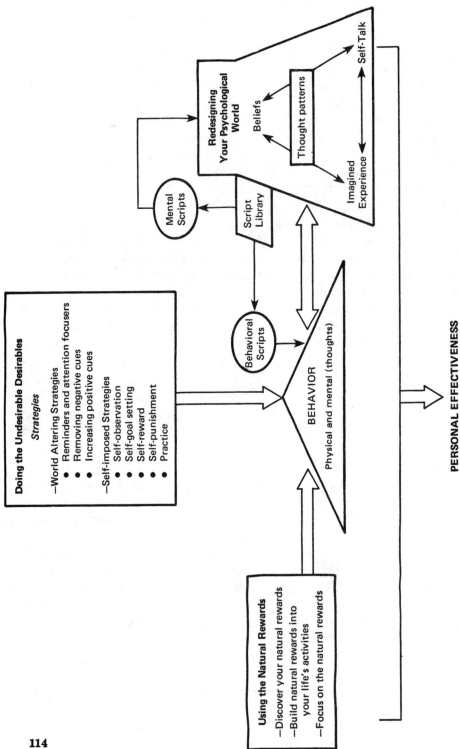

Doing the Undesirable Desirables

Strategies

—World Altering Strategies
- Reminders and attention focusers
- Removing negative cues
- Increasing positive cues

—Self-imposed Strategies
- Self-observation
- Self-goal setting
- Self-reward
- Self-punishment
- Practice

Redesigning Your Psychological World

Beliefs

Thought patterns

Self-Talk

Imagined Experience

Mental Scripts

Script Library

Behavioral Scripts

BEHAVIOR

Physical and mental (thoughts)

Using the Natural Rewards
—Discover your natural rewards
—Build natural rewards into your life's activities
—Focus on the natural rewards

PERSONAL EFFECTIVENESS

style and outlook. Ideally, this new pattern of self-leadership will be tailored to the unique values and needs of each of us.

In Chapter 6 examples were offered to illustrate how specific self-leadership strategies have been applied to deal with various challenges and problems. While these examples are informative, their shortcoming is that they cannot adequately illustrate the comprehensive self-leadership system outlined in Figure 7-1. Consequently, I will close this chapter with a fictitious case, inspired by my research and experience with self-leadership, designed to illustrate how a number of specific self-leadership strategies might combine to benefit a specific individual: one who, like you and me, is trying to cope effectively and enjoyably with the many challenges we face in the complex world in which we live. Such an excursion will, I hope, be instructive as well as entertaining.

A TALE OF SELF-LEADERSHIP

Tom Bigsby and Jim Wilks have never met; nevertheless their lives display some amazing parallels. They both work for regionally based, medium-size companies in a middle-management position. Each has a loving wife and a son and a daughter, aged 9 and 11, respectively. They both live in a nice suburban home in a large metropolitan area. In countless ways Tom's and Jim's situations are amazingly similar. The way they live their lives, however, differs like night and day.

A Day in the Life of Tom Bigsby

"What do you mean 'The budget is out of line'?" Tom blurted out angrily."You guys are just great! You want my department to achieve miracles, and you won't even provide us with the resources we need."

Don Greenlaw, the vice president of financial control, scowled back at Tom. "We don't want excuses here—we want performance; and as for your budget, it is just plain too extravagant."

"If we didn't clamp down on unreasonable budget requests like this one, we would have everyone feeding at the troughs too long," chimed in Bob Harris, the division manager, with an obvious tone of superiority in his voice.

Tom felt the veins bulging in his neck. It was obvious to him that the members of the budget committee had their minds made up before the meeting even started and were basing their judgments on a narrow-minded, conservative stance as they always did. He had had it this time. He rose to his feet to vent his rage and ...

"Honey, I wish you wouldn't gulp your food that way. You know the doctor said you need to learn to take things easier and relax."

"Never mind, Helen. I've got things on my mind," Tom snapped back. He leaned back stiffly into his chair a bit and let out a sigh. "This is going to be some day," he thought to himself miserably.

"Damn snow," Tom muttered as he scraped the ice off the windshield of his car. As he climbed in and started the engine, he felt symptoms of a nagging case of heartburn, apparently resulting from his hurried breakfast. Soon he was out on the expressway, on his way to work with the radio turned to the news, as usual. He occasionally commented sarcastically about "those incompetents in Washington," or complained about some other news issue as he weaved in and out of traffic in an attempt to hasten his drive to work. He did not notice the sunshine gleaming on the new-fallen snow that blanketed the trees, or the smiling snowman with hand raised in a gesture of friendly greeting next to a home visible from the road. Tom was deep in thought recounting the problems he had faced the previous day and visualizing distasteful results of the budget meeting he was to have that afternoon.

After parking his car, Tom quickly entered the tall office building of the beautifully landscaped complex in which he worked, occasionally muttering a hurried hello with a forced smile to persons he encountered. Tom felt that many of the people working for his company seemed pretty friendly, but he did not spend much time interacting on a personal basis. He felt the purpose of his job was clear—and that was to work. Personal conversation or interaction was not very important, including that which occurred over lunch, which he frequently skipped.

Tom threw a quick "hello" at his secretary and a nearby colleague as he promptly entered his office, removing his coat and hat as he did. He heard, but hardly noticed, the rather stiff, proper responses to his greeting in the wake of his departure. Tom sighed as he looked around the room. He did not like his office because it was here that he faced and suffered under the burden of troublesome problems. Soon he was shuffling through a pile of paper on his desk, scarcely noticing that his secretary had brought him his usual cup of black coffee.

The next two hours were mostly a blur to Tom as he repeatedly shifted his focus from one task to another. He was frequently interrupted by phone calls and employees with problems—mostly minor ones. Several stacks of reports and files had been pushed to the far side of his desk—some had been there for several days—while he worked on the immediate problems before him. It seemed he never really had time to think about or plan his actions.

Meanwhile, the snow continued to fall, and the view of the snow-blanketed countryside from his twelfth-story window was breathtaking. There was a shimmering frozen lake in the foreground and thick forests and rolling hills further away. Tom rarely looked up from his work, however, even when conversing on the phone. When he did have occasion to glimpse out the window, his thoughts were directed to potential problems with road conditions for his return trip home. "Damn winter," he muttered to himself.

At about 11:30 an employee in obvious distress entered Tom's office. "Mr. Bigsby, we're out of materials again," he complained. "And Supplies says there are none in Stock."

"Damn!" said Tom to no one in particular. "I haven't had time to look at the supplies situation. I'll try to arrange for a rush order, although I haven't had much luck in the past trying to push things through. Maybe I can use possible cancellations in the future as leverage if they don't come through for us," said Tom turning to the employee. "In the meantime, do what you can."

The employee left, frowning and obviously dissatisfied. At that moment the phone rang again. "Hello," Tom heard himself say as he picked up the receiver.

"Tom, I'm in a jam," said the voice on the line. "Your estimated sales report is long overdue, and the production folks say they can't wait any longer—they need the information today. Have you been working on it, Tom?"

"Uh, yes," said Tom a bit anxiously as he reached for one of the piles at the outside of his desk.

"I've got to have it today, Tom. I wish you would try to plan ahead a little more," said the voice.

"OK!" said Tom in an angry tone, and a bit too loud.

Tom worked through his lunch hour, as usual. He did not like working through lunch, but he felt the best way to get ahead in the company was to push hard. His intention this day was to get out the overdue sales projection report and the rush order on materials. He was distracted by several minor problems, however, and found he had made little headway by 2:00 that afternoon. Since the budget meeting was scheduled for 2:15, he began throwing some materials together.

Tom entered the meeting room in an uneasy, defensive frame of mind. He felt sure the budget committee intended to provide him with minimal support. His greetings to individuals present reflected this belief; his greetings were short and terse. The members of the budget committee responded in kind, and soon the atmosphere in the room was uncomfortably strained.

Tom delivered his presentation in about an hour and fifteen minutes. Several times he noted inconsistencies in what he said. Also, several issues were raised which he had not anticipated. His already strained manner of presenting his case became even more strained as time passed. Each time he encountered an issue he was not adequately prepared for, he tried to compensate by expressing his opinions especially emphatically despite the obvious lack of substantive support for these views. In desperation he tried to push his budget proposal through by sheer aggressiveness. Meanwhile he found that he was continually prodding himself with negative internal thoughts such as "Why did you say that? Now you really opened a can of worms, you dummy!"

By the end of the presentation Tom was noticeably exhausted and frazzled. The budget committee seemed to realize this because they were even a little gentle in the delivery of their negative feedback to Tom. In short, they told Tom he had not adequately thought through and documented his needs. They explained that they could not approve the budget in its current form, and recommended that he resubmit either a substantially reduced or a much better documented version in a week.

At this point Tom was no longer hearing all that was being said. He had, in essence, joined what he saw as his opposition by lambasting himself on the inside with negative internal self-statements: "I blew it again.....I never get anything right....."

"You don't seem to have a sense of direction in your department—no specific goals that you're working toward ..." the budget committee continued.

"Maybe I'm not cut out to be a manager," thought Tom. I just don't know what's wrong with me."

The meeting was over. Tom felt deflated, and the committee members seemed sorry and disturbed with what had transpired. One committee member with obvious good intentions singled Tom out privately as the others departed. "Tom, I've been in your shoes before. I know what you're feeling. I've found that going over my presentations ahead of time helps a lot. It can help in detecting problems and making adjustments before you do it for keeps. Also, you need to do a little thinking about the direction of your department. You need to spend some time planning."

"I don't have time to waste that way," Tom snapped back.

"Frankly, Tom, having to redo the budget is not going to save you much time either," the man responded with a smile he intended to be friendly and reassuring.

Despite the individual's good intentions, Tom was irritated. He left the meeting room in a huff.

After a couple more disorganized, hurried hours spent back in his office, Tom left the building, his briefcase full of troublesome problems that needed his attention. It had been another difficult day that had gone just as badly as he had expected. The snow had continued to lightly blanket the landscape and was now sparkling under the bright-orange setting sun. Laughter could be heard as a small group of employees playfully exchanged snowballs in the parking lot. Tom didn't hear. "Damn snow," he muttered as he swept the windshield of his car.

A Day in the Life of Jim Wilks

Jim's presentation to the budget committee had gone extremely well. "I appreciate your input," Jim was saying to the committee, "and your responsiveness to new ideas." He felt good about the strong support he had been given resulting from his effective budget proposal presentation. He had done a good job in providing convincing documentation and a well-thought-out, logical proposal for his requests.

Jim felt a sense of satisfaction surge through his body. He was impressed with the integrity and sincerity with which the meeting had been conducted. This was the kind of meeting Jim enjoyed— challenging him to refine his ideas, yet with an atmosphere of openness and flexibility.

Feeling exuberant, Jim rose to his feet to express his appreciation and ...

"Would you like some more coffee, dear?" asked Betty, Jim's wife.

"Uh, yes. Would you pour it into my thermos please?" he answered.

"You really seem to be deep in thought this morning. What's on your mind?" asked Betty as she poured the coffee.

"It's this budget committee meeting today. I think it's really going to provide me with an opportunity to state my case for the department to those that can make a difference. I expect it to be challenging, but I'm ready. I'm looking forward to it," responded Jim.

Jim settled back in his chair. "This is going to be some day," he thought enthusiastically.

After clearing the snow off the windshield of his car, Jim paused to toss a couple of snowballs at a nearby tree before climbing in and starting the engine. "This weekend will be a good time to take the kids sledding," he thought to himself. He imagined the kids laughing as they wooshed down a snow-covered hill.

Jim turned the radio on as he pulled onto the expressway. A newscast was on, so he turned to a station playing some quiet music. He liked to start the day with music rather than with the often bad news which he found sometimes had a negative effect on his thinking early in tne day. He would catch up with the newspaper and evening newscasts later on. After driving a few minutes through the scenic snow-covered landscape, Jim decided to get a little work done. He turned off the radio and proceeded to dictate a couple of memos to a tape recorder he had conveniently located next to him on the seat. He drove at a leisurely pace, sipping his coffee and enjoying the view.

When he reached his office complex, he felt relaxed and ready for the day. He strolled into his building, once again enjoying the snow-covered setting around him as he took some deep breaths of the clean, fresh air. He paused to deliver hearty greetings to fellow employees he passed. He enjoyed the people he worked with and found personal interactions to be a good source of information and ideas. He also realized that they helped establish important relationships that fostered cooperation when he needed assistance from others to get things done.

Jim stopped for a friendly chat with his secretary and a small group of colleagues who were conversing outside his office. After a short but pleasant and relaxed conversation, Jim entered his office. He smiled as he looked around the room that he had decorated (within a limited budget) to his personal tastes. He liked his office because it was here that he faced many stimulating challenges. He made a determined effort to keep his job enjoyable by working to mold it to his likes. He found there were many things to enjoy in his work if he looked for them—and he did.

Before beginning work on specific tasks, Jim took a note pad, eased back in his chair, and just thought for a bit while he savored a cup of coffee. He made a list of the more important activities that needed his attention during the day—"preparation for the budget meeting," he wrote on the pad, and added a star next to his notation for emphasis. The next couple of hours were spent working on the more important items on his list. He spent a good portion of his time reviewing the presentation he had planned for the budget meeting. He even spent some time rehearsing, quietly, the more important points he would make while also picturing a positive response and desirable outcome of the meeting.

As usual his secretary held his calls, allowing only the most important ones to go through to him. Jim had worked out a routine some months back where he would spend the better part of his mornings working on his more important activities, including planning. He designated a two-hour period after lunch as his "communication/troubleshooting" time. He spends this time discussing problems directly with employees and following up on phone calls. Employees know that only emergencies are to be brought to Jim's attention outside the two-hour period he has set aside after lunch. At first, employees resisted this limited open-door policy a little, feeling a bit shut out. But soon they came to look on it as an expression of confidence in their abilities. It was amazing how many problems they were able to solve on their own after limited access to Jim had been established. On the other hand, they knew Jim's doors were always open in the early afternoon.

While working, Jim would pause every so often to look at some of the pictures on his walls (many beautiful resort-type settings which he had either been to or wished to visit someday), or to gaze out the window. The snow was still falling outside, and the view of icy ponds and snow-covered trees from his tenth-story window looked to him like the most beautiful of Christmas cards come to life. He sometimes let his thoughts drift to a cup of hot chocolate in front of his blazing fireplace with one of his kids in his lap or some other pleasurable scene. He found short breaks such as these helped keep him relaxed and refreshed.

A small plaque he had placed on his wall caught his attention. It read, "There is nothing so powerful as the human mind well maintained and purposefully set into motion." "I need to do some more developmental reading," he thought, as though answering the plaque.

A determined smile came over his face as he gazed far off somewhere into the realm of possibility. Suddenly his attention snapped back to the present as he was struck by a powerful idea. He had been struggling for days on coming up with a more efficient way to process work going through the department. At this moment a new, innovative approach was clear in his mind. He quickly reached for a pad of paper (as he often did when a new idea came to him). "This will save us time and money," he thought enthusiastically. (The idea would later prove to reap these desirable results for the department and would play an instrumental role in his next promotion.)

About 11:30 an employee in obvious distress entered Jim's office. "Jim, the last shipment of materials we received is defective. We can't get any work done without materials."

"Call Frank Smith in Supplies," responded Jim in a concerned but controlled voice. "We have a couple days' worth of emergency materials in stock. In the meantime I'll call Fred Harris and have him rush us an order. We have a good working relationship, and I know he'll come through for me. Also, Dave, would you and the others take some time to think through a strategy for dealing with this kind of problem in the future? Maybe some kind of sample inspection could be made when the materials first arrive to help us detect problems *before* we're under the gun. Or maybe some other precautionary measure could be taken. Let me know what you think is best."

The employee left looking less concerned, and with a sense of responsibility in his stride. Things hadn't always worked out perfectly since Jim had become department manager, but the employees always knew where they stood and felt that they were a part of things. Jim certainly did not try to do everything himself nor be involved in all decisions concerning the department. The look of confidence and determination frequently seen on his employees' faces reflected the sense of responsibility they had come to feel under Jim's guidance.

The remainder of Jim's morning went well. Just before lunch he looked at his list of important things he wanted to work on during the day, and noted then with a sense of satisfaction that he had already finished most of them. He had a leisurely lunch with two of the employees in his department. He tries to arrange to go out with a couple members of the department twice a week, rotating who he goes with. He finds that the generally relaxed conversations away from the office are invaluable in keeping him abreast of the concerns of his workers and new developments in the organization. The lunches also foster good working relationships between Jim and members of the department.

After lunch Jim handled employee concerns and returned phone calls during his open office hours. This time is often rather hectic, but Jim tries hard to handle one matter at a time and to keep calm. He had arranged to shorten his office hours a little this day so that he would have a chance to collect his thoughts and briefly review his budget proposal one more time before the meeting. He made a list of pending matters and calls he had not been able to make today to be made in his office hours the following day. He usually found two hours a day to be more than adequate, so he felt confident he would catch up within a few days.

After a brief review Jim went to the meeting room early feeling a little nervous, but mostly confident and prepared. He delivered a friendly greeting to each budget committee member individually. Jim was pleased to have the opportunity to make the planned direction and resource needs of his department known to those individuals who held the "purse strings" in his company. He wanted to make the most of the time he had with them.

Jim's presentation lasted approximately one hour. It went very smoothly as planned—and Jim knew it. Even the issues raised by the committee were handled well. "I understand your concern about the increase in materials costs I've requested, and that's why I've prepared these charts," Jim was saying toward the end of the session. "As you can see, the expansion we've made in our product lines *as well as* increased materials costs make the request only a very slight increase over last year."

"Yes, I see," responded Stan Jones, the vice-president of financial control. "In that light, the request does seem very much in line."

"It appears you've really done your homework, Jim—I like the innovative changes you're establishing in your department," added Harry Willis, the division manager, who was obviously pleased.

Jim's budget was to be approved as proposed, and perhaps even more importantly, he had established improved professional relationships with very instrumental persons in his organization. He felt good about the support he had been given. His most important approval, though, came from Jim himself. He was liberal in his self-praise. The meeting was important; Jim had done well, and he let himself know it. "This is just the beginning," he thought. "I'm going to make things happen. I'm going to make a difference around here—I know I can do it."

After receiving some compliments from individual committee members, Jim returned to his office feeling good. He spent a couple of more hours working and made progress on some pending tasks, though he was a bit distracted in his elation. He left the office that day with no work to do. He is usually able to finish what needs to be done (those matters that could not be delegated) at the office, so he rarely does much work at home—although he often comes up with creative ideas for his department during his leisure hours, which he writes down on pads he has conveniently located in his home. Many of these ideas save him a great deal of effort later. He was ready to celebrate this evening. He found himself singing a couple of times while he reviewed his successes of the day, and once again enjoyed the snow-covered landscape. "What a day," he thought, "what a day."

THE TALE IN PERSPECTIVE

The case you have just read represents an attempt to illustrate two very divergent patterns of self-leadership under essentially identical conditions. Obviously, both individuals are trying very hard. Their general pattern of living, however, is leading to very different types of results. Simply put, Jim is exercising effective self-leadership à la this book—Tom is not. Jim is applying many of the strategies and techniques that have been suggested, and he is doing so in a way that is consistent with his own situation and personal makeup. He is controlling cues (having phone calls held and limiting office hours), for example. He is also monitoring his progress (self-observation) by using lists of pending tasks as a guide. Items on the list represent his goals for the day. Also, rehearsing his presentation apparently contributed significantly to his success at the budget meeting—the major challenge of his day.

A primary strength in Jim's approach is his overall constructive and positive orientation to thinking and behaving. For example, he is liberal in his use of self-rewards, both at the physical level (a good lunch after a hard morning at work, rewarding himself with rest breaks from time to time while he enjoys the pleasant pictures on his walls and the view out his window, planning to celebrate the day's success when he gets home) and the mental level (positive self-statements, imagining desirable experiences in the future). Perhaps even more importantly, Jim tries to build in, focus on, and otherwise experience the natural rewards of his work itself (surrounding himself with pleasant pictures on his office walls, he works in a steady and controlled, rather than frantic, haphazard style, and he purposefully seeks out the enjoyable aspects of his job).

Finally, and perhaps most importantly of all, Jim has adopted a desirable pattern of thinking. He has developed the ability to see through the often obstacle-laden exterior of challenges and to be especially responsive to the opportunities that are enveloped within. His orientation is to strive ever to achieve further advances and progress rather than to flounder and give in to formidable problems. His actions are controlled and well thought out, reflecting recognition of the obstacles that do exist. His course of action, however, is founded more on advancing toward existing opportunities rather than retreating from obstacles. Jim has indeed established a positive world, both psychologically and physically (e.g., through his actions toward others he has won their support when he needs it), in the way he lives his life.

Tom's mode of living, of course, reflects to a large degree an opposite pattern of self-leadership. Tom does not manage his behavior through the use of self-leadership strategies. Instead, he works in a disorganized, haphazard manner; in addition, he takes a basically negative, destructive stance toward his work. He focuses on the distasteful aspects of his job and keys his efforts primarily on the immediate obstacles he faces. He expects his work experiences and outcomes to be unpleasant—and so they are. What little time he *does* spend thinking about positive aspects of his job centers on future promotions or pay raises, and not on what he actually does. He has created a negative world for himself through his thoughts and his actions (e.g., he does not behave in a manner that helps ensure that he will have the support of others when he needs it). Tom has a self-leadership problem that will likely preclude his achieving personal and professional effectiveness unless he makes some major changes.

Do either of these two fictitious characters remind you of yourself? Perhaps you see a little of both Tom and Jim in you when you gaze into the mirror. The point is, you *do* have choices. These include both the way you choose to think about things and the way you choose to behave. This book offers a framework to help you to choose intelligently and to act on your choices wisely and efficiently.

Another type of fictitious character could have been developed—one who does not really try at all or, in essence, one who does not care about personal effectiveness. I'm assuming, however, that those who would read a book on self-leadership *do* care and *do* want to succeed (according to their own standards, of course). Consequently, the framework that has been presented is designed to provide insight into the choices you have concerning how you lead yourself to get more out of the effort you do exert and the types of overall self-leadership patterns that you can choose to establish for your life. If you are going to spend the effort to work and live, why not spend it wisely? Greater awareness and competence in applying the varied tools of self-leadership can be a powerful source of personal effectiveness. How are you spending your life? Are you moving ahead to benefit from the abundant opportunities that lie before you, or are you forever surrendering to obstacles along the way? The pursuit of self-leadership may well be the ultimate journey into yourself and your life. The destination is within your reach if you choose it to be.

8

The Journey Completed

"But who am I really?" the boy asked earnestly.

"Oh, now that is a difficult question," his father responded thoughtfully.

"It's more difficult than the questions you usually ask. In fact, it is about the most difficult question a man ever puts to himself, and then he searches for the answer the remainder of his life. And you have asked at such a young age."

"Then you don't know the answer, father," the boy muttered in a disappointed voice.

"No, son. The only one that can answer that question is you by the way you live your life. But perhaps I can help," he added in a reassuring voice.

"Come to the window and stand by me. What do you see?"

"I see the city, lots of people, cars, and other things," the boy said in a way that indicated he thought that it was obvious and the question was silly.

"Now look more closely, son. Look in all directions. What do you see?"

"I see lots of people living, I guess—some hills and a river. I see the world."

"Now you're getting closer, son. Look at the world long and hard all your life and eventually you will see and know yourself."

"How can that be, father? The world is not *me*, is it?"

"No, not exactly, son, but the world is largely a reflection of yourself—the way you see it, what you choose to look at, and how you choose to look at it, how you hold it deep inside yourself, and especially, what you make of it."

"You mean, I *make* the world?" the boy asked thoughtfully.

"Yes, you do as well as I and the people you see below."

Now the boy looked more earnestly out the window—he seemed to be seeing things he hadn't seen before: an old man walking with a cane, a gray bird gliding high in the clouds above, a piece of newspaper tumbling in the wind along the sidewalk, a little girl smiling while she did a messy job of eating an ice cream cone ... and gradually his focus seemed to broaden, and all these things began to somehow fit together. Slowly, with wonder, the boy thought he actually saw himself as though in a tremendous mirror—and he saw great possibilities for improvement and change, and especially for life.

We have now completed our journey, and I hope you have found it worthwhile. Before you lay this book aside, though, there are a few more ideas I would like you to consider. The following discussion will primarily address personal effectiveness—what it is and where it comes from. Also, as an added bonus, this closing chapter will briefly consider how to go about improving your world by contributing to the self-leadership of others, and some thoughts concerning self-leadership possibilities for the future.

PERSONAL EFFECTIVENESS

"Tell me, oh great one, why are you so triumphant and able in your every endeavor?" asked the admirer.

"It is because I believe that I am so," he responded in a powerful and confident tone of voice.

"But then tell me, great one, why do you believe you are so triumphant and able?"

"Because I *am*," he responded confidently.

At this the admirer scratched his head and thought for awhile. Then he asked, "Are you triumphant and able because you *believe* you are so, or just because you *are*?"

At this question he turned to the admirer with a faint trace of a smile on his face and a gleam in his eye that said the admirer had asked well. Then he said, "Yes, I have already told you so."

Some key self-leadership ideas have been presented in this book. It should be clear that in being effective self-leaders we need to recognize our interdependent relationships with the world in which we live as well as the way we influence ourselves directly. Indeed, we largely create our own personal world through our actions, and our world acts on us in countless ways. We also need to recognize the importance of our mental as well as our physical behavior. The observable actions we take to deal with problems and challenges are important, but our thoughts about these challenges (mental behavior) are just as important.

A wide range of approaches are available to us to effectively practice systematic self-leadership. Several techniques can be used, such as self-observation, self-goal-setting, and self-reward, to help us accomplish what we need to accomplish but have a hard time getting ourselves to do. We can also tap into the natural enjoyment of our challenges by building into our efforts, and otherwise seeking what we naturally enjoy about our activities. In addition, an especially powerful approach involves essentially redesigning our psychological world by developing desirable patterns of thought through the development of constructive beliefs, self-talk, and imagery. In particular, the design of effective behavioral and psychological scripts through which we act out much of our lives is an important vehicle for improving our self-leadership. Ultimately, all this should help us to become effective self-leaders and to achieve personal effectiveness.

But what *is* personal effectiveness? The answer to this simple but penetrating question will vary from person to person. Some basic aspects of personal effectiveness, however, can be distinguished for most situations. I would describe persons as being personally effective, for example, if they are able to reasonably accomplish what they set out to do with their lives, if they develop a healthy belief in their capabilities and value as persons, and if they develop a fundamental and reasonably stable satisfaction with life. To be personally effective, it would seem, is to believe we can deal with life's many challenges, and enjoy the successful handling of them.

One insightful view of the ingredients to personal effectiveness is encompassed in a concept known as "self-efficacy."[1] Self-efficacy is, in essence, our level of effectiveness in dealing with our world. More specifically, our perceptions of our own ability to deal successfully with and overcome situations and challenges we face in life can have a major impact on our performance. Available evidence indicates that our self-efficacy judgments influence the activities we choose to undertake or avoid, how much effort we expend, and how long we will persist in the face of difficult situations. Low self-efficacy judgments (e.g., beliefs that we lack the ability to deal with a difficult challenge) can lead us to exaggerate mentally our own deficiencies and the potential hazards of difficult situations.

This, in turn, can lead to anxiety and stress, and can detract from our performance. Our focus, for example, can too easily become that of obstacles and potential failure rather than opportunities and potentially successful alternative courses of action.

Perceptions of self-efficacy can indeed have an important influence on our personal effectiveness, but from where do our self-efficacy judgments come? Our self-efficacy judgments stem from several sources. One source is *observation* of the performance of others and their successes and failures. If we observe others, whom we can reasonably identify with, successfully overcome a particular challenge (earn a college degree, learn to skydive, etc.), our own self-efficacy judgments concerning the type of challenge involved should be enhanced. Another source is verbal *persuasion*. An inspiring speech by an athletic coach or a boss at work can sometimes convince the listeners that they can succeed and move them to execute the action necessary to do so. A third source stems from our perceptions of our *physical reactions* to a situation. If we feel calm and relaxed in the face of a challenge, for example, we are more likely to judge ourselves capable of overcoming the challenge than if we feel anxious and stressful.

Each of these sources of our self-efficacy perceptions is important and provides us with useful insight for enhancing our own personal effectiveness. If we seek out people whom we can identify with (people we believe are reasonably equal in ability to us), who use their talents well and overcome challenges they face, we provide ourselves with a good source for developing positive judgments of our own self-efficacy. Similarly, purposefully exposing ourselves to constructive verbal persuasion and gaining control over our physical reactions to difficulties can help us improve our self-perceptions, which should facilitate our performance. The most important source of perceptions of self-efficacy, however, is even more basic. It is simply our own *performance history*. If we experience successes in difficult situations, our perceptions of our self-efficacy will be improved. If we experience failure, they will be undermined.

This bit of information provides us with the basis for a very valuable insight—that is, that personal effectiveness leads to personal effectiveness. If we can master self-leadership skills such as those suggested in this book and consequently successfully take control of our lives and our situations, we can enhance both our current and future performance: our current performance through more intelligent, purposeful, and motivated immediate thought and behavior, and our future performance through enhanced self-perceptions of our personal efficacy or, in essence, of our own effectiveness. Thus, if we believe we are personally effective, we are likely to become even more so. The best way to develop a positive belief in our own effectiveness is by successfully handling the challenges we face in life. Mastery of systematic self-leadership skills can help us to achieve personal excellence in our own lives.

These ideas are illustrated pictorially in Figure 8-1. Self-leadership skills are an instrumental part of our level of personal effectiveness. They impact on our performance capability directly by helping to motivate and guide us in our immediate performances, and in future performances through the effect on our self-efficacy perceptions.

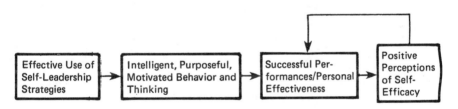

FIGURE 8-1. Self-Leadership and Personal Effectiveness

SOME ADDITIONAL THOUGHTS

Before closing this book, two "bonus" issues will be considered: first, some tips on developing the self-leadership skills of others, and second, thoughts on self-leadership issues of the future.

SuperLeadership: Leading Others to Lead Themselves[2]

"All right, Private Barnes. What's on your mind?"

"With all due respect, Sergeant Rogers, sir, I don't understand your leadership methods."

"O.K., Barnes—get it off your chest. What is it that's bothering you? You can speak frankly with me—you know that."

"Well, sir, it's just that we have one of the best outfits around. We always get a top rating and get the job done. But it seems we men do it all ourselves. Sure, you give guidelines, but you always want *us* to make the decisions. We are even supposed to reward and discipline ourselves! Don't get me wrong—I don't like being kicked around like most of the other sergeants do to get their men going; it just seems that you place too much responsibility on us enlisted men. After all, you're the officer and this 'your're your own sergeant in my outfit and I expect you to do a good job of making yourself the best soldier you can be' stuff you always give us seems funny, somehow. I mean, *you're* the leader, aren't you? Why do you want *us* to take all the responsibility for ourselves? It's like we're all supposed to be leaders around here. It's like we've *got* to be because you won't be one." Barnes paused nervously, his heart pounding, afraid he had said too much.

But Sergeant Rogers seemed unshaken. "Tell me, private. How do you and the men feel about yourselves?"

"Well, damn good, sir," he started cautiously. "We *ought* to—we're the best," he continued, now more confidently. "We pull together, supporting one another all the time. Yet each of us has a sort of individual dignity. We believe in ourselves and we do a hell of a job in our work."

"You were in the service a while before you got in my outfit, Barnes— how did you feel then?"

"Well, not too good, I guess. Being a soldier can kind of get you down. All I ever heard about is what I was doing wrong. I felt kind of like a rat in a maze with a hot electric wire chasing me." Then Barnes caught himself, "But at least the other sergeants would tell me what to do—they'd make the decisions and I would just do the work," he said quickly.

"Well, that's not the way I operate, private. I used to, but I don't anymore. Somewhere in my past I discovered the tremendous potential of every man, and I don't want to waste it anymore."

Now Barnes was in deep reflection. After a while a faint smile came to his face as though he had just discovered something new and wonderful. "I guess you lead us to lead ourselves, sir," he said (as much to himself as he did to Sergeant Rogers). "It's funny—you even got me to answer my own question," he said almost under his breath while turning to leave.

"Barnes," the sergeant called, stopping him in mid-stride, "you know I'm proud of you men."

"We know, sir," Barnes responded, "we are too, and I thank you for that."

The important interrelationship between ourselves and our world has been consistently discussed throughout this book. In addition, Chapter 4 suggested that for us to enjoy an activity naturally, one important aspect of the activity is that it provide us with a sense of purpose, which in many cases is encompassed in the notion of altruism. Here I would like to suggest a powerful method for improving our personal world and achieving a sense of altruistic purpose at the same time: the practice of SuperLeadership. Super-Leadership can be described as the process of helping others to develop and practice systematic effective self-leadership. It involves bringing out and stimulating the development of personal effectiveness of people we associate with. While Henry Sims and I wrote an entire book on this topic entitled *SuperLeadership* (see note 2), the idea of leading others to lead themselves is a unique and compelling perspective on the broader topic of leadership itself—here are a few simple ideas and a procedure which will be suggested as a starting point.

Henry Sims and I suggested a procedure for managers to help their employees to manage themselves better.[3] It consisted of three primary components: setting a good example, guidance, and reinforcement of self-management. The first step is displaying self-leadership skills in your own behavior. It's been said that "actions speak louder than words," and in this case that old adage is especially true. By displaying systematic self-leadership practice in your behavior (setting goals for yourself, purposefully making your work naturally enjoyable, seeking out opportunities rather than shrinking in the face of obstacles, etc.), you are serving as an effective, concrete model and stimulus for others to do the same.

Providing an example for others, however, is not enough. They will also likely need a considerable amount of specific guidance. Here encouragement and instruction in self-leadership skills are important. The goal is to get the target of your efforts thinking and behaving in a self-leading manner appropriate to that person. One useful approach to accomplishing this end is to ask appropriate questions: Do you have any goals for your efforts? How well do you think you did and how do you feel about that? What aspects of your work do you enjoy? How could you make it more enjoyable? What kinds of opportunities are you pursuing right now? Are you looking for new ones?

When they *do* start putting self-leadership techniques into practice, suggestions and feedback are important. In particular, positive reinforcement of self-leadership effort is crucial (e.g., "I'm glad to see you setting goals for yourself—this should help you better accomplish what you set out to do"; "Your outlook has really improved—I can tell that opportunities, rather than obstacles, are your primary motivators now"). It's important to remember, though, that the aim is to shift the leadership function to the other person(s). SuperLeadership ultimately means assisting others to become their own primary source of goals, rewards, work enjoyment, opportunities, and so forth in a way that is best suited to them. In our book *SuperLeadership* we provided specific strategies for developing self-leadership in individuals as well as in teams and in broader organizational cultures (see note 2). Whether the others are work subordinates, a spouse, a child, or a friend, ideally the aim should be to help them become all they are capable of becoming in a way that will give them the most personal satisfaction and growth.

It should be apparent from the "Tale of Self-Leadership" in Chapter 7, that a lot of Jim's self-leadership effectiveness (and Tom's ineffectiveness) stems from the way he leads his subordinates. Jim is an effective self-leadership model and allows his employees the freedom to exercise initiative. To emphasize further Jim's SuperLeadership style, let's return to his case as the tale continues.

THE TALE CONTINUED

In the months that passed under Jim Wilks' leadership, the department underwent many significant changes. Jim's innovative ideas often led to refinements in work processes, and efficiency continued to rise. These were the obvious changes, but the most important ones were a bit less obvious and invariably involved the growth of his people. In fact, many of Jim's subordinates who previously had never been viewed as particularly innovative or self-directing had gradually evolved into very creative, independent workers. Many of Jim's better ideas began with suggestions from his employees, or in some cases the whole ideas would be designed and implemented by one or more of his employees with little or no involvement from Jim. And Jim was quick to give them credit in front of their peers as well as their superiors.

"Good morning on this beautiful, sunny day," Jim said to his staff at the beginning of one of their weekly department meetings. "I'd like to officially introduce Dave Henry to you, although I believe most of you have already met him. He joined us at the end of last week just having received his degree from City U. I, for one, am extremely pleased that Dave has decided to work with us and I hope that each of you will help Dave during his transition.

"And, now, I believe it's Nancy's turn to conduct the meeting. So I'll stop rambling and turn the floor over to her," Jim finished.

The meeting was fairly typical, led by one of Jim's subordinates who rotated this responsibility. It began with a few minutes of brainstorming of department work improvements, followed by practical discussion of department challenges that needed to be addressed. They were referred to as challenges or opportunities because Jim, early on, after he had taken the department head position, had convinced his staff that problems were really opportunities that had not yet been adequately explored. Jim had in fact changed a lot of the old language in the department so that it projected more positive imagery. The transition occurred largely as a result of the example Jim had set in the early meetings of his tenure in the department. As a consequence, over time, the meetings themselves had become more pleasant and productive and on this particular day, the tone of the meeting was the same with one exception.

"I know I'm pretty new around here, Bob," Dave, the new employee, was saying to one of the department staff, "but I think there may be some real problems in the implementation phase of your plan."

"I appreciate your interest, Dave, and I invite your input to help me work out some of the details. Also, Dave, you may find this a little strange but we don't use the word 'problem' much in meetings around here any more. We've decided it has a negative effect on our thinking, so we try to talk in terms of 'challenges' or 'opportunities'."

"Oh," Dave responded in a slightly surprised tone, "sorry about that," as he turned toward Jim with a mildly confused look on his face

"Don't worry about it," Jim answered for Bob. "We know it takes some getting used to but we think you'll like the positive atmosphere that's created by managing the language we use so that we create constructive imagery for problem solving or what we refer to as opportunity generation."

In fact, the whole meeting seemed a little strange to Dave, who couldn't understand what was so bad about identifying problems with ideas that were being considered in the department. After all, the first step in effective decision making he had been taught at City U is to identify the major problems that exist. Over time, though, he became a real supporter of the unique subculture in the department that reinforced employee initiative and being your own leader much more than avoiding mistakes. Dave found this took a lot of the negative stress out of the work and made it a fun environment to work in. In fact, there was a kind of informal slogan in the department that said,

"If you're not making any mistakes, you're probably not trying hard enough." It's not that making mistakes was encouraged, but exercising initiative and taking reasonable chances were expected in the department as a natural part of each person's contributing their full enthusiastic (not just compliant) potential.

Dave especially learned this lesson the day he lost a major order from a potential client because he was late in delivering a price bid. His bid was late because he had taken a lot of time to develop a unique service arrangement tailored to the client's needs, the key to his proposal. After explaining the situation to Jim, he braced himself for the logical chewing out he would receive after such a screwup.

"How do you like your work here so far?" Jim began.

"Uh, fine," Dave responded sounding a little confused about the question.

"Have you been redesigning your job to fit your interests and strengths?"

"I'm not sure. I haven't really thought about it," Dave said sounding even more confused and unsure how to answer.

"Well, I hope you have been," Jim said. "I want you to get a real kick out of your work and to be able to put your best foot forward.

"Now, as for your proposal, why did you develop this new service plan?" Jim continued.

"To provide the best package for the client," Dave responded, "and the most attractive overall product for getting the contract."

"Why do you want the contract? What are you working toward?" Jim asked next.

"Well, I'm hoping to increase our contract volume for this product line," Dave answered.

"Good, I like people to be goal-oriented. Have you thought about how much of an increase your working toward?"

And so the conversation continued: "How well do you think your doing?" "Do you celebrate your successes, reward yourself for when you do well?" And as they talked, Dave was really getting a sense of Jim's leadership style. Jim wanted his people to think, not only about how they did their work, but why. But most of all, he just wanted his people to think about the choices they constantly faced and made. He wanted them to think about their personal effectiveness and skill in leading themselves, not just their technical proficiency.

"But, still, surely the lost contract was a significant failure and sooner or later the conversation will have to get around to my botched performance and a justifiable reproach from Jim," Dave thought to himself.

Jim continued to examine the report that Dave had prepared for the client for what seemed an awfully long time. Dave was sure Jim must be gathering his feelings of dissatisfaction for a pointed reprimand. "Congratulations," Jim said finally. "This is the most innovative service plan I've seen in this department thus far, and it capitalizes on our resource strengths very well. This is really going to generate a lot of business for us with our clients in the future."

Now Dave looked really confused. "You mean I've lost a very large order with a very important potential new client, and you're not mad?"

"Gee, Dave, you sound almost disappointed. You see, I don't believe in chewing someone out for initiative and hard work. Besides, I think what you see as a short-term failure is going to generate tremendous opportunities for us in the long run."

"Well, the client was really pleased with the plan and told me that although it wasn't in in time to be considered for this order, he felt confident that we would be getting orders from them in the future."

"You see, I told you," Jim responded with a businesslike smile that indicated he was already anticipating the future benefits for the department.

"I guess you're right," Dave said with a slight smile now himself, although he still looked bewildered as he turned to leave Jim's office.

"By the way, Dave," Jim stopped him in midstride. "Don't expect me to chew you out every time you make a mistake. I suspect you'll know when you've screwed up and I figure it's your job to keep yourself on track as well as your peers. Give your work your best shot making full use of your talents and I'm confident that you'll win a lot more than you lose. The longer you're around here I think you'll find we all operate that way and it works."

And in the days ahead, Dave found Jim's observation to be true indeed. Dave, in fact, became one of the best self-leaders in the department, following Jim's example but also developing his own system of self-direction.

Once, several weeks later, when asked by a top corporate executive what made Jim such an effective department manager, Dave's response was quick and enthusiastic. "He lets us lead ourselves," Dave said simply. "And it's not hard to do around here with the example he sets and the encouragement he gives us," he continued. "I am still getting used to his style. I mean he still surprises me. Sometimes I think I've really blown it on a project and he praises me for my initiative, hard work, and creativity, even though things did not work out the way we hoped. Other times I think I've done something just the way he would have, the way I think he would want me to, and he sounds kind of disappointed that I didn't come up with a new, better way that is all my own. He likes us to get the credit and to have the satisfaction of succeeding—that's what pleases him."

Dave continued: "I guess you could say he's helped shape a uniquely effective little world here where yes men and women are not allowed, a place where people really grow and develop and have a lot of fun because they have the satisfaction of testing the limits of their creativity and ability. It's funny, we are all leaders in this department. I'm still not sure how he's done it, but in my book he's the best. He's the best leader I've ever seen. And it seems like he is the best because he doesn't need to be. He wants us to fully share his leadership role and his glory by being our own ultimate leaders—each one of us. And he wants each of us to be the best self-leaders we can be."

The Tale in Perspective Continued

SuperLeadership is a very real leadership alternative. Modeling, encouraging, guiding, and reinforcing self-leadership are the key ingredients. Jim does this, and his employees benefit and so does his organization.

Jim clearly models effective self-leadership in his own behavior and serves as a credible example of personal effectiveness. He encourages his people to make choices that contribute to their personal growth, effectiveness, and satisfaction. He guides them in their development with strategic use of questions that stimulate self-leadership thinking. And he reinforces constructive self-leadership practice, sometimes even when immediate performance does not measure up. He does this because he realizes that in the long run, fully developed, enthused, self-led workers will win a lot more than they lose, and a lot more than if they are just compliant followers of his commands.

Finally, Jim has developed a subculture in which self-leadership can feed on itself. One in which each person is challenged to be all he or she can be and know that what is expected is nothing less. Jim has, in essence, facilitated the emergence of an almost idyllic world for fully utilizing human resources. Yet it's a world that is very achievable for those leaders who are willing to let their people share in the process and to learn the exhilaration of mastering the leadership of themselves.

Future Directions in Self-Leadership

He looked carefully into the eyes of the very intelligent being from another world. Then he asked, "Do you think we on earth are very primitive?"

"No," the being answered, "At least not in all ways."

"Then you do think we are primitive in *some* ways," he continued, intending the statement as a question. But the being did not respond. "I mean," he continued, "we have explored the universe and we have harnessed the power of the atom. We have made great advances in the control of disease and we have even mastered the art of manipulating genes for improving our race in future generations. Given all this, how can you think we are primitive in some way? In what way?" he asked now in an irritated voice.

"Yes, you have explored much," the being responded. "In some ways you have even surpassed the beings of my planet in your mastery of the physical world, though not many."

The man shook his head in acknowledgment. "But also you have neglected much."

"What do you mean? What have we neglected?" the human asked.

"Your focus has been outward. You have neglected what is within. It's as though you have tried to master living but have forgotten to explore life."

"What do you mean? We have made great advances in biology and medicine. We are closer to controlling life itself than we have ever been!" he responded a bit too emphatically.

"I'm not talking about your physical bodies," continued the being. "I'm talking about the core of life, the mind and the spirit."

"But we've made great advances in psychology and psychiatry, and tremendous discoveries regarding the functioning of the brain," exclaimed the human.

"The brain is but a part of the physical body—a sort of computer to be used in dealing with the world. Life is more. You have spent so much time trying to control the world that you have forgotten the mastery of yourselves."

"But science indicates that we are ultimately what the world makes us through evolution, socialization, and so forth. It is the world that makes us what we are, isn't it?" the man asked, now thoughtfully—unsure, as though he was beginning to understand. "Isn't that the true order of things and why we must focus our major efforts on the world?"

"Only if you choose it to be," the being answered simply. "We of my planet have chosen to focus our primary efforts inward instead of outward. We have discovered that the world is largely what we make it. But we must first make something of ourselves before we can make the world. Yes, you have surpassed us in some things: weaponry to destroy and instruments to squeeze from the physical world the wants of the body. In this way you are advanced. But you have neglected the most powerful resource you have—the power of the mind, the core of yourselves."

As a final consideration, it is useful to look for a moment into an imaginary crystal ball of self-leadership possibilities for the future. My belief is that the major breakthroughs in the next few decades will be in an arena that we have generally thought of as a bit strange and almost mystic. I am referring to the capabilities and powers we hold deep within ourselves but which are largely unexplored and uncharted as of yet: the powers of the mind.

An interesting and insightful book on the subject is Barbara Brown's *Supermind*.[4] She argues that the brain and the mind are really two distinct realities. Considerable effort has been spent exploring the physical functioning of the brain: electro-chemical impulses, left and right hemisphere functioning, and so forth. Our understanding of the almost mystical powers of the mind, however, seems to have been reserved for usually questionable and unscientific witnessing from persons encountering "strange" experiences that defy scientific explanation: people lifting cars off endangered loved ones, miraculous physical healings through effort of mind, premonitions, and ESP.

Yet the evidence is vast enough and often credible enough to warrant a belief that mind power is a powerful, perhaps the most powerful, untapped resource. Take, for example, the mounting evidence regarding biofeedback—a process by which persons are connected to sophisticated monitors of the human bodily functions which provide feedback regarding physical processes that, in the past, were considered beyond the arena of intentional control. Experience with biofeedback has shown that not only can we control bodily functions such as heart beat, blood pressure, and skin surface temperature, but also brain wave activity. The point is that through a learning process, humans can learn to control processes of the body (even brain activity) that for years were believed to be beyond control.

In this book I have attempted to balance the emphasis placed on physical behavior and thought. Both play an important role in the total self-leadership picture. In the future, however, self-leadership advances will need to travel beyond the level of our current conscious awareness capability into the largely unconscious processes and powers of the mind. The purpose is not so much to use the mind as a window to our "true personalities," as Freud and other psychologists have done in the past, but instead as a resource for gaining advanced self-leadership capability and personal effectiveness. Preliminary journeys have begun into this exciting new frontier. The ultimate in personal effectiveness of the future will likely be an advanced state of integration and harmony of our world, our behavior, our conscious thought processes, and the deeper recesses of the mind.

ENDNOTES

[1] See Albert Bandura, "Self-Efficacy Mechanism in Human Agency," *American Psychologist*, 37 (1982), 122–147.

[2] This is the title of the book by Charles C. Manz and Henry P. Sims, Jr. (Englewood Cliffs, N.J.: Prentice Hall, 1989; New York: Berkley [paperback], 1990) on the subject of leadership of others to become self-leaders.

[3] See Manz and Sims, *SuperLeadership*; and Charles Manz and Henry P. Sims, Jr., "Self-Management as a Substitute for Leadership: A Social Learning Theory Perspective," *Academy of Management Review*, 5 (1980), 361–367. See also Donald Meichenbaum and Roy Cameron, "The Clinical Potential of Modifying What Clients Say to Themselves," in M. J. Mahoney and C. E. Thoresen, *Self-Control: Power to the Person* (Monterey, Calif.: Brooks/Cole, 1974), which provided us with the basis for the procedure.

[4] Barbara B. Brown, *Supermind: The Ultimate Energy* (New York: Harper & Row, 1980).

Epilog

Having completed my writing, I have found it interesting to read back through what I have written. It has been a useful time of reflection regarding my own self-leadership. I have not yet mastered all the self-leadership strategies suggested in this book, but I have successfully used many of them and I am continually working on others. I have come to realize that I wrote this book as much for myself as I did for others. The significant time and energy I have spent over the past few years studying, thinking, and reading about self-leadership necessitated that I attempt to coherently organize a workable framework for application. In a way, the framework I have presented represents a personal goal for my own style of living.

Through my reflection, I have also come to another perhaps even more important realization: that while I already knew I have much to learn from others, I now see that I also have a great deal to learn from myself. The rather philosophical thought has occurred to me that possibly there is a basic truth regarding our own lives deep within us, and this truth specifies our most suitable style for living. Maybe that's a large part of what self-leadership is all about: seeking that part of ourselves that best defines a satisfactory fabric with which to weave our life experiences into a personally effective life. The ideas I have presented in this book (most of which have been successfully applied in multiple settings) represent my best attempt at providing a vehicle to help you (and myself) embark on such a journey.

Index